COMMON ENTRANCE • KEY

CE

English

Elly Lacey

Boost

GALORE PARK

AN HACHETTE UK COMP

About the author

Elly Lacey is Head of English at Newton Prep School in London. She has taught English to children from aged 8 to 18 but her particular passion is teaching at Key Stage 3. After a prior career in PR and marketing, Elly rediscovered her love of teaching while volunteering on a trainee scheme in New York. Once she returned to the UK, she embarked on her teaching career in a secondary school in West London. In the classroom, she endeavours to build children's confidence and love of English through creative activities and cross-curricular links, all inspired by the texts on the curriculum. Outside of education, Elly always makes time for her love of theatre (both on and off the stage) which from time to time infiltrates her teaching practice too. Elly is a first-time author and brings plenty of fresh ideas for teaching to *English for Common Entrance 13+*.

Every effort has been made to trace all copyright holders, but if any have been inadvertently overlooked, the Publishers will be pleased to make the necessary arrangements at the first opportunity.

Although every effort has been made to ensure that website addresses are correct at time of going to press, Galore Park cannot be held responsible for the content of any website mentioned in this book. It is sometimes possible to find a relocated web page by typing in the address of the home page for a website in the URL window of your browser.

Hachette UK's policy is to use papers that are natural, renewable and recyclable products and made from wood grown in well-managed forests and other controlled sources. The logging and manufacturing processes are expected to conform to the environmental regulations of the country of origin.

Orders: **Teachers**, please contact Hachette UK Distribution, Hely Hutchinson Centre, Milton Road, Didcot, Oxfordshire, OX11 7HH. Telephone: (44) 01235 400555. Email: primary@hachette.co.uk. Lines are open from 9 a.m. to 5 p.m., Monday to Friday.

Parents, Tutors please call: (44) 02031 226405 (Monday to Friday, 9:30 a.m. to 4.30 p.m.). Email: parentenquiries@galorepark.co.uk

Visit our website at www.galorepark.co.uk for details of revision guides for Common Entrance, examination papers and Galore Park publications.

ISBN: 9781398321571

© Hodder & Stoughton Limited 2021

First published in 2021 by Hodder & Stoughton Limited
An Hachette UK Company
Carmelite House
50 Victoria Embankment
London EC4Y 0DZ

www.galorepark.co.uk

Impression number   10 9 8 7 6 5 4 3 2 1

Year   2025 2024 2023 2022 2021

Cover image by Barking Dog

Illustrations by Aptara Inc.

Typeset in India by Aptara Inc.

Printed in Italy

A catalogue record for this title is available from the British Library.

MIX
Paper from
responsible sources
FSC™ C104740

Contents

Text credits

p.10 Gino, A. (2015). George (Scholastic Gold). Scholastic Inc.; **p.17** Robert Frost (1923). New Hampshire: A Poem with Notes and Grace Notes. Henry Holt and Company; **p.18** Heaney, S. (2009). Death of a Naturalist. Faber & Faber; **p.20** Bill Bryson (2006). The Life and Times of the Thunderbolt Kid. Doubleday; **p.26** Sedgwick, M. (2010). Floodland. Hachette UK; **p.33** The Newcomer by Brian Patten; **p.34** Ark by Simon Armitage; **p.36** Adrienne Matei, (2020). Your polyester sweater is destroying the environment. Here's why. © Guardian News & Media Limited; **p.42** Isaac Asimov, (1950). I, Robot, HarperCollins; **p.44** Ray Bradbury, (1953). Fahrenheit 451, HarperCollins Publishers; **p.50** Ian McWethy, (2015). The Internet is Distract—OH LOOK A KITTEN!: A Short Comedy, Playscripts; **p.53** UK adults 'spending a quarter of their waking lives online due to lockdown', The Independent, Published on Wednesday 24 June 2020; **p.60** Ayesha Harruna Attah, (2020). The Deep Blue Between, Pushkin Press Limited; **p.64** David Morton, (2018). The Wider Earth, Nick Hern Books; **p.68** Down and Out in Paris and London by George Orwell, US rights held by Peter Frasers & Dunlop; **p.74** Malorie Blackman (2008). Noughts & Crosses. Penguin Random House; **p.83** Carol Ann Duffy. 'Rapture', published in 2005 by Picador; **p.85** Hannah Devlin (2019). What is love – and is it all in the mind?. Guardian News & Media Limited; **p.92** Michael Crichton, (2012). Jurassic Park, Penguin Random House; **p.99** Evan Placey, (2017). Jekyll and Hyde, Nick Hern Books Limited; **p.102** THE INVENTION OF THE VACUUM CLEANER, FROM HORSE-DRAWN TO HIGH TECH (2020); **p.108** Zana Fraillon, (2016). The Bone Sparrow, Hachette UK; **p.110** Onjali Q. Rauf, (2018). The Boy At the Back of the Class, Hachette UK;

p.114 Refugees by Brian Bilston; **p.118** 5 MINUTES WITH...MAGIC MAGID by Living North, 2019; **p.124** Annabel Pitcher, Silence is Goldfish (2015). Hachette; **p.131** From PBS Winter Choice The Perseverance, published by Penned in the Margins 2018; **p.132** From Selected Poems by Tony Harrison, published by Penguin Books, Ltd. Copyright © 1984; **p.134** Sinéad Burke, Break the Mould: How to Take Your Place in the World, ISBN 9781526363343, © 2020 Hachette UK; **p.142** Sally Gardner, Julian Crouch, (2012). Maggot Moon, Bonnier Publishing; **p.147, 148** David Haig, (1997). My Boy Jack, Nick Hern Books; **p.151** Zlata Filipovic, (1995). Zlata's Diary A Child's Life in Sarajevo, Penguin Random House; **p.158** Jewell Parker Rhodes. (2018). Ghost boys. Hachette UK; **p.160** Catherine Bruton (2019). No Ballet Shoes In Syria. Nosy Crow; **p.165** From The Black Flamingo by Dean Atta published by Hachette ISBN: 9781444948585; **p.166** Langston Hughes, "Harlem" from The Collected Works of Langston Hughes. Copyright © 2002 by Langston Hughes. Reprinted by permission of Harold Ober Associates, Inc.; **p.168** Reprinted with permission from the rightsholder. Speech given at the UN Women HeForShe campaign on 20 September 2014.

Photo credits

This book is available as an eBook on our new online platform, Boost.

Introduction

English for Common Entrance is for pupils in Key Stage 3 at a junior school, where pupils sit ISEB Common Entrance at the end of Year 8.

Most Preparatory School pupils will sit two papers: a reading paper (either Foundation Level or Paper 1) and a writing paper (Paper 2). Some pupils will sit a CASE or scholarship paper.

The ability range of pupils taking part in English 13+ Common Entrance is wide-ranging so individual schools must determine which of the reading papers each pupil will sit. This book includes examples and skills appropriate for Foundation, Paper 1, Paper 2 and CASE, as well as for the Key Stage 3 National Curriculum. As a course, English for Common Entrance 13+ is devised to be diverse and multi-faceted and to be used alongside class readers and the study of media text topics.

In Common Entrance **Paper 1**, pupils will answer questions on reading texts, which may take the form of a prose passage, a poem or an excerpt from a play (Foundation candidates will answer on a prose text). We have captured the breadth of these forms and styles in the chapters with a diverse range of authors and texts taken from a variety of historical eras and genres, from recent newspaper articles to Victorian science-fiction and a modern Bildungsroman to Shakespeare. Not only will this prepare the pupils for the exam but also broaden their reading experience. At the end of each chapter, the pupils will be offered ways of widening their reading around the chapter's theme.

When encountering this range of texts, pupils will be encouraged to explore and discover the social and historical contexts in which the authors were writing. Many of the texts focus on important and current themes such as gender, climate change and people of different abilities, which will ignite discussion, understanding and empathy with others. We have included many cross-curricular links within the activities so pupils can apply knowledge and skills from different subjects.

The questions are organised into three sections, which are graduated in complexity in terms of skills and length of answer. In this book, we call them **Questions**, **Writing questions** and **Extended questions**. In the accompanying **Answers** (available separately as a PDF download) you will find full answers to all the questions, including the extended reading response questions. The Answers also contains lesson planners which capture the activities and skills coverage of each chapter.

In **Paper 2**, pupils will have a choice of which writing task to tackle. These could range from a story to descriptive writing, or from a persuasive task to a letter giving recommendations.

In this book we have provided examples of these types of writing and writing frames for a range of tasks, as well as encouraging pupils to apply and hone their writing skills through a variety of other tasks in 'Putting pen to paper'. The accompanying Answers also contains full sample responses for these writing tasks.

Questions

These are short-answer reading comprehension questions.

Writing questions

These are questions requiring a more complex written answer to reading comprehension extracts.

Extended writing questions

These are questions requiring an extended analytical or creative response to reading extracts.

The mechanics of language are introduced in an integrated way in all the chapters but also as discrete spelling and punctuation tips. There is a **Glossary** of terms to refer to, which presents all key technical terms explained throughout the book as one reference tool.

Last but not least, there is the **Exam skills** chapter, which offers full guidance on the questions pupils will face in the exam by providing sample responses and tips on improving responses to the different question types. In this section, pupils will also find further advice and tips on writing for different purposes and in different forms. Additionally, there is some language support for common errors in writing. This section might be referenced and used during the whole course or towards the end, as pupils start to focus more on exam preparation.

Notes on the features in this book

Language focus

This feature explains the language, imagery or vocabulary the writer has used, helping the pupil to think analytically about the text.

Grammar/punctuation focus

Here, a key grammatical feature or punctuation rule is dissected, modelled and pupils are then able to try it for themselves in a focused activity.

Drama focus

In this feature, pupils are able to explore a text or a text's themes using active dramatic techniques.

Speaking and listening focus

An opportunity to hone those vital speaking and listening life skills through debate, active listening, discussion and sight-reading.

Review your writing

Offers the opportunity for a pupil to self- or peer-assess their extended writing piece with guidance.

Book review

An activity at the end of each chapter to inspire peer recommendations and also a chance to commit to the optional ISEB reading certificate.

Text features

This feature highlights the specific elements of a text type, especially its organisational features, to help pupils think analytically about the text.

Talking point

A chance to discuss and empathise with the wider themes and issues which occur during the chapters.

Aims

Gives a handy overview of the chapter's aims at the start of each chapter, including the main foci for reading, writing, language, drama and speaking and listening.

Context

Background to the context in which each extract is set or written is offered before pupils read the text.

About the author

The writer is introduced before each text so the pupils can gauge when they were writing, what interests them and their background.

Punctuation – spelling tips

These provide extra advice about spelling patterns and punctuation rules.

Research

These questions offer pupils the opportunity to find out more about certain aspects of a text, especially its context, and practise research skills.

Read more

A recommendation of what to read if pupils are interested in that particular text's theme or author's style.

Wider reading

At the end of each chapter there is a list of books and authors that write about similar themes or in the same genres. More complex reads are highlighted with *.

1 Growing up

Aims

- **Reading focus**: Inferring meaning and unlocking poetry
- **Writing focus**: Narrative and autobiographical writing
- **Speaking and listening focus**: Summarising and recall
- **Language focus**: Effects of simple sentences, sound devices, iambic pentameter and humour
- **Drama focus**: Scriptwriting

Context

Growing up is hard to do. But to use the words of Peter Pan (who found it very hard to grow up himself), it's an 'awfully big adventure' too. Adults can get nostalgic about 'the best years of your life' and even writers can be a bit sentimental when it comes to growing up. But sometimes, just sometimes, it's worth listening to their youthful experiences because (who knows?) maybe you'll hear something you needed to.

In this chapter, we'll be exploring what it means to grow up through the eyes of various characters, each with their own growing pains. You will share part of your life story before turning an event from it into an exciting narrative.

About the author

Alex Gino is an American writer who was born and raised in New York, even though they have lived across the country. They are **genderqueer** (a person who does not subscribe to conventional gender distinctions but identifies with neither, both, or a mix of male and female genders). They use singular 'they' pronouns when referring to themselves, because it is gender neutral.

George was their first novel. In 2016 the novel won the Stonewall Book Award, which recognises exceptional literary merit relating to the gay/lesbian/bisexual/transgender experience.

When people look at George, they see a boy. But she knows she's a girl. She knows she's really Melissa. Along with bullies, homework and school plays, she is trying to work out how to tell her family she is **transgender** (a person whose sense of personal identity and gender does not correspond with their birth sex). In this extract, she has just arrived home to read her hidden stash of magazines.

George

George picked up an issue from last April that she had looked through countless times before. She browsed the busy pages with a crisp flip-flip-flip that stirred up the faint smell of paper.

She paused on a photo of four girls at the beach. They modelled
5 swimsuits in a line, each striking a pose. A guide on the right-hand side of the page recommended various styles based on body type. The bodies looked the same to George. They were all girls' bodies.

On the next page, two girls sat laughing on a blanket, their arms around each other's shoulders. One wore a striped bikini; the other
10 wore a polka-dot one-piece with cut-outs at the hips.

If George were there, she would fit right in, giggling and linking her arms in theirs. She would wear a bright-pink bikini, and she would have long hair that her new friends would love to braid. They would ask her name, and she would tell them, 'My name is Melissa'. Melissa
15 was the name she called herself in the mirror when no one was watching and she could brush her flat reddish-brown hair to the front of her head, as if she had bangs.

George flipped past flashy ads for book-bag organisers, nail polish, the latest phones and even tampons. She skipped over an article on how to
20 make your own bracelets and another on advice for talking to boys.

George's magazine collection had started by accident. Two summers ago, she had noticed an old issue of *Girl's Life* in the recycling bin at the library. The word girl had caught her eye instantly, and she had slipped the magazine in her jacket to look at later. Another girls' magazine
25 soon followed, this time rescued from a trash can down the block from her house. The very next weekend, she had found a denim bag at a yard sale for a quarter. It was just the size of a magazine and had a zipper along the top. It was as if the universe had wanted her to be able to store her collection safely.

30 George settled on a two-page spread about FRAMING YOUR FACE WITH MAKE-UP. George had never worn make-up, but she poured over the range of colours on the left side of the page. Her heart raced in her chest. She wondered what it would feel like to really wear lipstick. George loved to put on Chapstick. She used it all winter, whether or
35 not her lips were really chapped, and every spring she hid the tube from Mom and wore it until it ran out.

George jumped when she heard a clatter outside. She looked out of the window to the front door directly below. No one was in sight, but Scott's bike lay in the driveway, the back wheel still spinning.

40 Scott's bike! That meant Scott! Scott was George's older brother, a high school freshman. The hair on George's neck stood up. Soon, heavy footsteps climbed the stairs to the second floor. The locked bathroom door rattled. It was as if Scott were rattling George's heart inside her rib cage.

45 Bang! Bang Bang!

'You in there, George?'

Alex Gino

Questions

1 What person is the extract written in? (1)
2 What does George imagine wearing if she were with the girls in the magazine? (1)
3 How has George's brother, Scott, arrived home? (1)
4 What is the noun that alerts George to Scott's arrival? (1)
5 The effect of the short sentence 'The locked bathroom door rattled' is to ease tension. True or false? (1) **FP**

Grammar focus

Simple sentences

The way we use sentences in our writing can change how it's read. A sentence must have a **subject**, a **verb** and sometimes an **object**. For example:

Her heart raced in her chest.

subject   verb   object

A simple sentence is built from this minimum. Simple sentences may well be simple but they're very effective. You may spot more of them in contemporary texts. Here are some examples:

- Give facts: *Paris is the capital city of France.*
- Tension: *I opened the door. She was there.*
- Emphasise points: *We must change!*
- Make the meaning easier to understand: *It was a wonderful day.*

Write six simple sentences, aiming to create different effects.

About the author

Charles Dickens (1812–1870) was a British writer and social critic. He wrote some of the most famous novels of the Victorian era but also wrote non-fiction about his travels, and particularly about London. His tough childhood influenced his writing and his charitable work, and he reflected Victorian society's whims and ills in his writing, including the distinct social-class differences.

Context

Dickens' writing often includes characters from all social classes. At the start of *Great Expectations* (1861), Pip is living in poverty with his sister's family on the Kent marshes. First, he encounters a frightening escaped convict; next he is invited to play at the grand Statis House. This is occupied by Miss Havisham, a spinster stuck in her past, and her young ward, Estella, who put him through some social tests.

In this extract, Pip is desperate to impress Miss Havisham and Estella when they first meet but, as they play cards, he feels out of place.

Great Expectations

'Let me see you play cards with this boy.'

'With this boy! Why, he is a common labouring-boy!'

I thought I overheard Miss Havisham
5 answer – only it seemed unlikely –
'Well? You can always break his heart.'

'What do you want to play, boy?' asked Estella of myself, with the greatest disdain.

'Nothing but beggar my neighbour, miss.'

10 'Beggar him,' said Miss Havisham to Estella. So we sat down to cards.

It was then I began to understand that everything in the room had stopped, like the watch and the clock, a long time ago… As Estella dealt the cards, I glanced at the dressing-table again, and saw that the shoe upon it, once white, now yellow, had never been worn. I glanced down
15 at the foot from which the shoe was absent, and saw the silk stocking

on it, once white, now yellow, had been trodden ragged. Without this arrest of everything, this standing still of all the pale decayed objects, not even the withered bridal dress on the collapsed form could have looked so like grave-clothes, or the long veil so like a shroud.

20 So she sat, corpse-like, as we played at cards; the frillings and trimmings on her bridal dress, looking like earthy paper. I knew nothing then, of the discoveries that are occasionally made of bodies buried in ancient times, which fall to powder in the moment of being distinctly seen; but, I have often thought since, that she must have looked as if the admission

25 of the natural light of day would have struck her to dust.

'He calls the knaves, Jacks, this boy!' said Estella with disdain, before our first game was out. 'And what coarse hands he has. And what thick boots.'

I had never thought of being ashamed of my hands before; but I began

30 to consider them a very indifferent pair. Her contempt was so strong, that it became infectious, and I caught it.

She won the game, and I dealt. I misdealt, as was only natural, when I knew she was lying in wait for me to do wrong; and she denounced me for a stupid, clumsy labouring-boy.

35 'You say nothing of her,' remarked Miss Havisham to me, as she looked on. 'She says many hard things of you, but you say nothing of her. What do you think of her?'

'I don't like to say,' I stammered.

'Tell me in my ear,' said Miss Havisham, bending down.

40 'I think she is very proud,' I replied, in a whisper.

'Anything else?'

'I think she is very pretty.'

'Anything else?'

'I think she is very insulting.' (She was looking at me then, with a look

45 of supreme aversion.)

'Anything else?'

'I think I should like to go home.'

'And never see her again, though she is so pretty?'

'I am not sure I shouldn't like to see her again, but I should like to go

50 home now.'

'You shall go soon,' said Miss Havisham, aloud. 'Play the game out.'

I played the game to an end with Estella, and she beggared me[1]. She threw the cards down on the table when she had won them all, as if she despised them for having been won of me.

55 'When shall I have you here again?' said Miss Havisham. 'Let me think…come again after six days. You hear?'

'Yes ma'am.'

Charles Dickens

1 She beat him at the card game called 'Beggar my Neighbour'.

Questions

1 Who is the narrator? (1)
2 What is the definition of 'disdain'? (1)
3 What does Pip call the knaves? (1)
4 In your own words, explain what Pip has 'caught' in lines 30–31. (2)
5 Which adjective best describes Pip overall? (1)
   a naïve
   b confident
   c shy
   d arrogant **FP**

Punctuation tip: colons and semicolons

Colons can replace a 'because' and semicolons can replace an 'and'.

Life is like a box of chocolates: (because) you never know what you're going to get.

This is my box of chocolates; (and) I ate them all.

Talking point

Our memories can be like time travelling but nothing quite beats the sci-fi version where characters can control every second. Miss Havisham has tried to control time but has not succeeded, so how would you do it? Use the questions below to discuss time in small groups.

● When does it feel like time is dragging for you? When does it feel like it's speeding by?
● If you could, under what circumstances would you stop time?
● If you could go back in time within your own life, where and when would you go, and why?

Research

Charles Dickens' life is just like a **plot** of one of his novels. Use the following questions to research his life.

● Where did Dickens work as a child and why did he work there?
● What social issues did he write about?
● What house did he buy later in his life that was part of his childhood? Why do you think he bought it?

Writing questions on *George*

1 Why do you think George reads the magazines? (2)
2 In your own words, explain why George thinks the 'universe' wanted her to have the denim bag. (3)
3 Read lines 37–44. Find two ways in which the author uses language to show George is scared. (4)

Writing questions on *Great Expectations*

1 What impressions does Pip have of Estella at the end of his visit? (4)
2 Miss Havisham is stuck in her past. In lines 11–19, how does the language show the reader this? (4)
3 How can you tell Pip is a young boy in this extract? Use evidence from the text to support your ideas. (4)

Speaking and listening focus
Summarising

Summarising is a great skill to practise verbally because as you grow up, you'll have to **summarise** your experiences in interviews, biographies and business pitches.

In groups of three, take turns as The Summariser, The Listener and The Fact-checker.

The Summariser will have one minute to summarise one key event in their life so far. Maybe it'll be an important trip, the birth of a sibling or playing in their first football match. Here are some tips for summarising:

● Plan and practise what you are going to say before you say it.
● Take pauses to breathe – summarising is not about speed; it's about precision, especially when someone is listening.
● Be precise and stay on topic. For example, there's no need to explain what you had for breakfast on that day in much detail.

The other two members of the group must listen carefully because after The Summariser has finished, The Listener will then recall the main points to The Fact-checker so that they can check their listening skills are top notch.

Take turns until everyone has had a chance to summarise, listen and fact-check.

Thematic focus

The extracts were written over 100 years apart so their plots, characters and writing styles are going to be very different. By recognising key elements of texts from different eras, we can become better readers and writers.

Contrast the two extracts by completing the table below. A few examples have been added to get you started:

How and why do the characters feel pressure to behave in a certain way?		Who and what are the characters intimidated by?		How do we feel about the characters as readers?	
Extract 1	Extract 2	Extract 1	Extract 2	Extract 1	Extract 2
	Visiting grand house	Scott – older brother			Sympathy

Extended writing questions

You will now be writing an extended answer about an extract. Write your answer in three PEEA paragraphs, using evidence from the text to support your ideas. (See page 179 in the Exam skills chapter for an explanation of the PEEA technique.)

Here are some tips for writing extended answers:

- Read the questions carefully.
- Use the three foci in your topic sentences for the three paragraphs.
- It might help you to find your evidence for each before you start writing.
- Use connectives like 'and', 'furthermore', 'however' and 'additionally' to expand your explanations.

1 Extract 1 comes from the first chapter of *George*. How does the author, Alex Gino, introduce us to the protagonist?

   You should focus on word choice, the character's actions and the character's thoughts.

OR

2 How does the author of Extract 2, Charles Dickens, make this a memo-rable scene?

   You should focus on the characters, language and structure.

OR

3 Retell the story in Extract 2 from Estella's point of view.

   You should explore:

   - her observations of Pip
   - her feelings about Miss Havisham
   - whether she would like to see Pip again or not.

Language focus
Unlocking poetry

About the author

Robert Frost (1873–1963) was an American poet who was actually published in Britain before America. He often wrote about rural American settings, using them to examine philosophical ideas. At the time he was writing, the world was going through huge changes as a result of industrial and communication revolutions, the World Wars and political upheaval. His poems may seem rustic and quaint but look a little further and you will find deeper meanings.

Robert Frost's short poem, 'Nothing Gold Can Stay' (1923), is packed with hidden meaning. Let's unlock this poem using the advice above and considering our chapter theme.

Read more

If you like this poem and its sentiment, try reading the coming-of-age novel, *The Outsiders* by SE Hinton. This poem recurs throughout the plot as it's very important to a couple of the characters.

Context

Poems can seem challenging. Even though their brevity can be useful under timed writing conditions, more often than not, we think they're holding some kind of hidden meaning that we're not allowed to know, like a locked treasure chest and we don't have the key. But there are reading strategies we can use to unlock poems:

● Look at the title – poems have titles for a reason. Take a close look at it before you read the poem.
● Connotations – these are associations we make with words or phrases or symbols. For example, yellow makes us think of happiness, grey of sadness.
● Put in your own words – rephrase a line in your own words. Does it reveal something by using synonyms or exploring the different meanings of words?
● Comparisons – look at the comparisons the poet uses in similes or metaphors. What do they suggest?

'Nothing Gold Can Stay'[1]

Nature's first green[2] is gold,[3]
Her hardest hue to hold.[4]
Her early leaf's a flower;[5]
But only so an hour.
Then leaf subsides to leaf.[6]
So Eden sank to grief,[7]
So dawn goes down to day.
Nothing gold can stay.[8]

Robert Frost

1 The title is ambiguous but it's about something leaving or not lasting, even though it's made of the most durable metal.

3 Connotations of gold are precious, wealth, perfection, beauty. Can you think of others?

4 Put a line into your own words – the most difficult colour to hang on to.

5 Comparison – of a leaf to a flower. Flowers are more beautiful and more fragile than leaves. They don't last very long, so they're more precious too.

6 Connotations – these few lines refer to time and things changing.

7 Comparison – Eden refers to the biblical Garden of Eden, a perfect place that then was ruined.

2 Connotations of green are fresh, new, youthful, spring. Can you think of others?

8 It's the title again! Own words: Nothing lasts forever. How does this idea link to this chapter's theme of growing up?

About the author

Seamus Heaney (1939–2013) was an Irish writer who grew up in Northern Ireland and won the Nobel Peace Prize for Literature in 1995. He appreciated writers who wrote about their local and native background. He was also a translator and his translation of the epic Anglo-Saxon poem 'Beowulf' is well-renowned. As you will notice, 'Blackberry Picking' (1966) discusses childhood through the lens of nature too. The link is the innate theme of the growth of both childhood and the natural world.

'Blackberry Picking' requires some unlocking. Use the tips from 'Nothing Gold Can Stay' to help you unlock how blackberry picking represents childhood for Seamus Heaney.

1 A dark fairy-tale character with blood on his hands from murdering his wives.

'Blackberry Picking'

Late August, given heavy rain and sun
For a full week, the blackberries would ripen.
At first, just one, a glossy purple clot
Among others, red, green, hard as a knot.
5 You ate that first one and its flesh was sweet
Like thickened wine: summer's blood was in it
Leaving stains upon the tongue and lust for
Picking. Then red ones inked up and that hunger
Sent us out with milk cans, pea tins, jam-pots
10 Where briars scratched and wet grass bleached our boots.
Round hayfields, cornfields and potato-drills
We trekked and picked until the cans were full,
Until the tinkling bottom had been covered
With green ones, and on top big dark blobs burned
15 Like a plate of eyes. Our hands were peppered
With thorn pricks, our palms sticky as Bluebeard's[1].

We hoarded the fresh berries in the byre.
But when the bath was filled we found a fur,
A rat-grey fungus, glutting on our cache.
20 The juice was stinking too. Once off the bush
The fruit fermented, the sweet flesh would turn sour.
I always felt like crying. It wasn't fair
That all the lovely canfuls smelt of rot.
Each year I hoped they'd keep, knew they would not.

Seamus Heaney

Questions

1 In what season is the poem set? (1)
2 In lines 1–4, what are the two things the freshly picked blackberries are compared to? (2)
3 What language technique is used in the phrase 'summer's blood' (line 6)? (1)
4 What is the definition of 'hoarded' (line 17)? (1)
5 What does the speaker always feel like doing when the blackberries become sour? (1)

Language focus
The power of sound

Consider these three categories of poetic devices:

Types of poetic devices			
	Imagery – devices we can 'see'	Sound – devices we can 'hear'	Structure – devices that build the poem
Some examples	Metaphor	Onomatopoeia	Rhyme
	Simile	Alliteration	Rhythm
	Personification	Assonance	Enjambment

In 'Blackberry Picking', sound devices begin with the use of **onomatopoeic** words (words that sound like the word they're describing) like 'tinkling'.

More subtly, the effect of **alliteration** (the **repetition** of consonant sounds at the start of consecutive or close words) depends on the consonant used. For example, the double 'f' of 'fruit fermented' makes the fruit sound unpleasant.

Assonance (the repetition of vowel sounds in words that are close together) is also used, for example, in 'on top big dark blobs'. It slows a reader down by drawing out the vowel sounds, just as the speaker is enjoying eating the berries!

Text features
Rhythm and meter

Iambic pentameter is a type of **rhythm** famously used by William Shakespeare. Even though it's been used for plays and poetry, it is supposed to recreate the natural pattern of speech, making it easy to remember. Lines of iambic pentameter should have ten syllables and five alternate stresses. For example:

*Late[1] **August**, **given**[5] **heavy rain** and **sun**[10]*

Try reading the line aloud, clapping on each syllable. You should clap ten times. Now read it aloud, while clapping on every other syllable. You should clap five times.

Decide if it works for every line of the poem.

Questions

1 Read lines 3–8. How does the poet create a vivid description of the freshly picked blackberries? (4)
2 Read lines 8–16. How does the poet make blackberry picking seem like a sensory experience from his childhood? (4)
3 Considering language, structure and tone, what are the differences between the first stanza and the second stanza? (6)

About the author

Bill Bryson is an award-winning American–British writer who is well known for his hilarious and engaging style. He has written travel books about the UK, America, Australia and Africa, as well as books on science and history.

His childhood memoir, *The Life and Times of the Thunderbolt Kid* (2006), displays all his usual idiomatic style and laugh-out-loud anecdotes as he recalls his childhood in 1950s Middle America.

The Life and Times of the Thunderbolt Kid

The only time I have ever broken a bone was also the first time I noticed that adults are not entirely to be counted on. I was four years old and playing on Arthur Bergen's jungle gym when I fell off and broke my leg.

Arthur Bergen lived up my street, but was at the dentist or something
5 when I called, so I decided to have a twirl on his new jungle gym before heading home.

I don't remember anything at all about the fall, but I do remember very clearly lying on damp earth, the jungle gym now above and around me and seeming awfully large and menacing all of a sudden, and not being
10 able to move my right leg. I remember also lifting my head and looking down my body to my leg which was bent at an unusual – indeed, an entirely novel – angle. I began to call steadily for help, in a variety of tones, but no one heard. Eventually I gave up and dozed a little.

At some point I opened my eyes and a man with a uniform and a peaked
15 cap was looking down at me. The sun was directly behind him so I couldn't see his face; it was a hatted darkness inside a halo of intense light.

'You alright, kid?' he said.

'I've hurt my leg.'

He considered this for a minute. 'You wanna get your mom to put
20 some ice on it. Do you know some people named…' – he consulted a clipboard – '…Maholovich?'

'No.'

He glanced at the clipboard again. 'A.J. Maholovich. 3725 Elmwood Drive.'

'No.'

25 'Doesn't ring a bell at all?'

'No.'

'This is Elmwood Drive?'

'Yes.'

'OK, kid, thanks.'

30 'It really hurts,' I said. But he was gone.

I slept a little more. After a while Mrs Bergen pulled into the driveway and came up the back steps with bags of groceries.

'You'll catch a chill down there,' she said brightly as she skipped past.

'I've hurt my leg.'

35 She stopped and considered for a moment. 'Better get up and walk around on it. That's the best thing. Oh, there's the phone.' She hurried into the house.

I waited for her to come back but she didn't. 'Hello,' I croaked weakly now. 'Help.'

40 Bergen's little sister, who was small and therefore stupid and unreliable, came and had a critical look at me.

'Go and get your mom,' I said. 'I'm hurt.'

She looked at my leg with
45 comprehension if not compassion. 'Owie,' she said.

'Yes owie. It really hurts.'

She wandered off, saying, 'Owie, owie,' but evidently took my case no further.

50 Mrs Bergen came out after some time with a load of washing to hang.

'You must really like it down there,' she chuckled.

'Mrs Bergen, I think I've really hurt my leg.'

'On that little jungle gym?' she said, with good-natured scepticism, but came closer to look at me. 'I don't think so, honey.' And then abruptly:
55 'Christalmighty! Your leg! It's backwards!'

'It hurts.'

'I bet it does, I bet it does. You wait right there.'

She went off.

Eventually, after quite some time, Mr Bergen and my parents pulled up
60 in their respective cars at more or less the same moment. Mr Bergen was a lawyer. I could hear him talking to them about liability as they came up the steps. Mr Bergen was the first to reach me.

'Now you do understand, Billy, that technically you were trespassing…'

Bill Bryson

Questions

1 To whom does the new jungle gym belong? (1)
2 Read lines 8–9. How is the jungle gym described effectively? (2)
3 In the context of the extract, what does 'novel' mean (line 12)? (1)
4 Who is the first person to come across the fallen Billy? Use evidence from the text to support your answer. (2)
5 What has Mrs Bergen come out to do when she finally notices Billy's leg? (1)

Research

Here are some final questions to guide your research into the extracts and writers in this chapter:

1 'Bildungsroman' is a type of literary genre, but what does it mean?
2 Can you find any books that fit into that genre?
3 What countries has Bill Bryson written about in his travel writing?
4 What other subjects does Bill Bryson write about? Is there anything you didn't expect?

Text features

Narrative drive

Even though it's non-fiction, it feels like fiction. As a reader, we're engaged from the first line that hooks us in and kept interested throughout as various 'characters' come and go. This is called narrative drive. All the while our 'hero' is stranded, broken-limbed on the grass. In autobiographical writing, you can identify narrative drive in the following areas:

- Language – the gripping vocabulary or imagery and how the characters speak.
- Structure – how the story develops from start to finish, including any moments of tension.
- **Characters** – how they're described, which characters become the most important, who is constant and who comes and goes.
- Tone – how tone changes throughout the story, the balance of dialogue and description, and how punctuation changes tone.

 # Language focus

It's the way he tells 'em!

Humour is very important to Bill Bryson's writing style, but how does he do it?

- **Tone** – the fact that he never shows outrage towards the adults in this story, as its protagonist or narrator, makes it funnier.
- Asides are always used in plays for the characters to tell the audience something secret. By using parentheses in writing, you can achieve the same thing. For example, 'my leg which was bent at an unusual – indeed, an entirely novel – angle.'
- **Timing** and pace are important when performing comedy. In writing this is usually achieved by following a long sentence with a short sentence, just like a joke's punchline.
- **Rhythm** should be considered in prose as well as in poetry. For example, the power of three or repetition can help develop the hilarity. In pairs, read aloud the exchange between Billy and the first person to find him to see its effect.
- Last but not least, the reader's **expectations** must be turned upside down for laughs. Did you really expect a four-year-old boy with a broken leg to be left for that long and then be accused of trespassing?

 # Drama focus

Using one of the extracts from this chapter as inspiration, write a short script using the same plot, characters and including key words or phrases.

Perform it to the rest of the class without telling them what extract you have chosen.

Did some groups choose the same extract? Did you perform the same characters in different ways?

Writing task

Using Bill Bryson as your inspiration, you are going to write a humorous narrative based on an event that's happened in your life. It will be autobiographical but remember, in an exam, the marker won't necessarily know if you have exaggerated or elaborated.

Humour can be difficult to write but use the tips on the previous page to consider the following:

- tone
- asides
- timing and pace
- rhythm
- subverting expectations.

The power of three

Also look out for the number **three** in humour. Comics and humorous writers often use three of something for the perfect amount of hilarity. For example, there are three people who come across Billy before someone realises how badly he is hurt.

Use the plan below to help you structure your humorous narrative. Bill Bryson's examples are included to inspire you.

Beginning: the build-up Narrative hook. Set the scene. Lull the reader into a sense of normality and that everything will be fine!	*Don't trust adults* *Introduce situation (visiting Arthur but he's at dentist) and setting (jungle gym)*
Middle: the event The longest part. What happened. Lots of detail. Reactions to the event.	*Fallen off jungle gym – description, asides* *First person doesn't realise I'm badly hurt, asks where someone lives* *Mrs Bergen arrives (really happy) and doesn't realise I'm hurt* *Arthur's sister sees me but she's too young to help* *Mrs Bergen comes out again and realises how bad it is, then calls parents*
Ending: the punchline What happened afterwards. Could be a twist to subvert expectations. Rhetorical questions and short sentences helpful here!	*Mr Bergen and parents arrive* *Mr Bergen says I'm trespassing*

Time to write

Write a humorous narrative based on an event that's happened in your life.

Putting pen to paper

Now have a go at one of the writing tasks below. Use ideas from the first writing task or go it alone.

1. Write a narrative with the title 'Laugh Out Loud'.
2. Write a short story about a joke that goes wrong.
3. Write about a time that made you laugh.

Peer review (editing/drafting)

Reviewing your writing

Swap your writing with a partner. Read each other's work carefully, looking at:

- whether it makes you laugh – identify the devices your partner used to make it funny.
- the way ideas are expressed – are they clear?
- how the narrative is structured – do the ideas link well?

Find two positive things that would improve the writing in your view. Share these with your partner.

Edit your work, considering these changes and correcting any spelling or punctuation errors.

> ### Wider reading
>
> If you want to read more coming-of-age novels, have a look at these brilliant books:
>
> - *Martyn Pig* by Kevin Brooks
> - *I Capture the Castle* by Dodie Smith
> - *The Adventures of Huckleberry Finn* by Mark Twain*
> - *Crongton Knights* by Alex Wheatle
> - *Chinese Cinderella* by Adeleine Yen Mah
> - *David Copperfield* by Charles Dickens*
>
> *Choose these titles for a more challenging read!

Book review

Prepare a short review for a book you have read recently. It might be one from the wider reading list above.

Remember to include three things about your chosen book which made you want to read on.

Share your review with a partner. What do you think of their book recommendation?

2 Our planet

Aims

- **Reading focus**: Inferring meaning through language features
- **Writing focus**: Persuasive and discursive writing
- **Speaking and listening focus**: Debate
- **Language focus**: Persuasive language techniques, irony and voice, direct speech
- **Drama focus**: Creating different characters

Context

Our precious planet is under threat from climate change but by working together we can make a difference. The predictions can sound daunting but there are things we can do: turning off lights, recycling and reusing our waste or even riding a bike or walking to school instead of taking a car. Our beautiful planet can be protected. The solution to the problem lies with us.

The writers in this chapter highlight the issues that we're facing, the consequences if we don't take action but also the beauty of our planet and its inhabitants. By the end of this chapter, you will write your own piece about why and how we should all be striving to save the planet. And you'll not only read the opinions of humans but of animals as well, because it's their planet as well as ours.

About the author

Marcus Sedgwick is an award-winning British writer, illustrator and musician who now lives in the French Alps. *Floodland* (2000) was his first novel and is a cautionary **dystopian** tale about climate change.

In *Floodland*, the sea level has risen. England is covered in water and the city of Norwich is an island. Zoe, the protagonist, remembers the time she is left behind in the confusion when her family tries to leave for the safety of the mainland.

Floodland

After the water came, Zoe and her parents had tried for years to stick it out in Norwich, along with another hundred or so. After a while, they realised they were fighting a losing battle, and that the sea was not going to stop rising. Zoe's mum was ill, too. She seemed to have 5 a sickness that came and went and had lasted for weeks. They'd had enough.

Back then, there were still fairly regular supply trips from the mainland. A big ship used to bring as much food as could be spared and anchor half a mile offshore. After rowing in with the supplies and 10 sharing them out, the captain would ask if anyone wanted to leave. Usually there would be one or two more people ready to go to the mainland.

But just when Zoe's parents had decided to get off the island, the boat stopped coming. Instead of the usual four or six weeks, three 15 months went by before it reappeared. Finally it slipped into view late one night, as if the captain knew there would be trouble. By now a lot more people than usual wanted to get off the island. There was confusion; it was dark, and a terrible fight broke out to get aboard the two tiny rowing boats. Zoe helped her dad get her mum on board one 20 of the boats, just as it was pulling away from the shore. It was already dangerously overloaded. Two men were trying to push each other out of the boat, even as the oarsman took his first strokes. One of them succeeded in shoving the other out. There was only time and room for Zoe, or her dad, to jump in.

25 She saw her dad hesitate. She had never seen that before; he always seemed to know what to do. She could see him torn between getting in the boat with his sick wife, or putting his daughter in with her.

Zoe looked at the other boat; there was still a little room to be had. She decided to help her dad; to make the decision for him.

30 'You go with Mum; she needs you,' she yelled.

'No!' said her dad.

'I'll get the other one.' She pointed. 'I'll see you on board the ship.'

'No,' he said, 'You get in the boat...'

Then the oarsman noticed them. 'Only one of you!' he shouted. 'And
35 make it quick! The ship's already full! We're leaving!'

He started to pull hard now.

'Dad! It's only as far as the ship. I'll see you there...'

Still he hesitated. Zoe forced her decision. She backed away from the
boat.

40 'I'm going for the other one. Get on board, Dad! Quick!'

She saw the relief in her dad's face as he climbed aboard from waist-
deep water.

'Zoe...well, go then!' he shouted. 'Get in the other boat! Hurry, Zoe!'

Zoe turned and saw with horror that the other boat was already
45 leaving. More people were arriving from the town, too, sensing this
could be the last chance to get away. They headed for the boat Zoe was
making for. She ran across the slimy muddy shore, and tried to climb
in over the stern of the boat, then someone hit her on the chin. She fell
back dazed in the mud, and watched as the boats moved away towards
50 the lights of the ship.

Suddenly she realised that she was being left behind. Her dad thought
she was on the second rowing boat, that he would see her on the ship.
She knew the captain wouldn't come back for her. With all these people
there would only be another fight. She had to let her dad know now,
55 before the rowing boats reached the ship. She tried to shout, but her
voice was weak with exhaustion.

Then she thought she heard her dad call to her.

'Zoe? Are you there?' came his voice through the dark.

'Dad, I'm here! Come back! Get them to come back! Please!'

60 She thought she was yelling, but in reality she could only manage a
whisper. There and then a numbness came to her. Her brain closed in
on itself, blocking out the full impact of what happened. She blacked
out, the sea lapping at her legs.

Marcus Sedgwick

Read more

If you enjoyed Marcus Sedgwick's writing, try out his novel *Snowflake, AZ* too. It's about illness – humans' illness but also the planet's. This time there's no water and it is set in the Arizonia Desert.

Questions

1 What does the big ship bring to the island? (1)
2 How long has it been since a ship has been seen before this night? (1)
3 What member of Zoe's family is already in the boat? (1)
4 Why doesn't Zoe get in the other boat? (1)
5 Zoe ends up in the forest at the end of the extract. True or false? (1)

Punctuation focus
Speech punctuation: Who said that?

Direct speech can be effective in creating characters, adding pace, tension and plot but you must set it out correctly! It's all about making it clear for a reader, so your priority should be to open and close your **inverted commas/speech marks**. That way a reader knows when the talking starts and finishes.

In handwritten work, it's better to use double inverted commas/speech marks so that it's not confused with other punctuation marks. Look at the example below:

1 Every line of direct speech must end with a punctuation mark within the speech marks. When there is a comma, what follows is called a **reporting clause**.

4 This is **split direct speech**: the sentence is split by a reporting clause.

> 'You go with Mum; she needs you,[1]' she yelled.
>
> [2] 'No!' said her dad.
>
> 'I'll get the other one.'[3] She pointed. 'I'll see you on board the ship.'
>
> 'No,'[4] he said,[5] 'You get in the boat…'
>
> Then the oarsman noticed them. 'Only one of you!' he shouted[6]. 'And make it quick! The ship's already full! We're leaving!'

2 New line for a new speaker.

3 Sentence is finished so it's a full stop followed by a capital letter for the **verb phrase**.

5 In a line of split direct speech like this one, remember to include a comma after the reporting clause.

6 Make sure your punctuation within your speech reflects the verb phrase in your reporting clause. In this case the exclamation marks show he is shouting.

Write six lines of dialogue between three characters that continues the extract from *Floodland* following the rules above. You might want to start like this:

'Help her up, Joe,' called a voice Zoe seemed to recognise.

She croaked in reply, 'Hel-hel-hello.'

About the author

Jack London (1876–1916) was an American writer and social activist. He was a prolific writer of novels, short stories and magazine articles. He became an international celebrity for his books but the inspiration for his most famous works, *The Call of the Wild* (1903) and *White Fang* (1906), came from his time panning for gold in Canada during the Klondike Gold Rush.

In *The Call of the Wild*, Buck was a beloved, pampered pet in sunny California when he was stolen to work as a sled dog in the inhospitable setting of Yukon, Canada. The novel is written from his point of view as he becomes increasingly wild, acting on his natural instincts around the pack of sled dogs, including his greatest rival, Spitz.

The Call of the Wild

At the mouth of the Tahkeena, one night after supper, Dub turned up a snowshoe rabbit, blundered it, and missed. In a second the whole team was in full cry. A hundred yards away was a camp of Northwest Police, with fifty dogs, huskies all, who joined the chase. The rabbit sped down
5 the river, turned off into a small creek, up the frozen bed of which it held steadily. It ran lightly on the surface of the snow, while the dogs ploughed through by main strength. Buck led the pack, sixty strong, around bend after bend, but he could not gain. He lay down low to the race, whining eagerly, his splendid body flashing forward, leap by leap,
10 like some pale frost wraith, the snowshoe rabbit flashed on ahead.

All that stirring of old instincts which at stated periods drives men out from the sounding cities to forest and plain to kill things by chemically propelled leaden pellets, the blood lust, the joy to kill – all this was Buck's, only it was infinitely more intimate…

15 […] There is an ecstasy that marks the summit of life, and beyond which life cannot rise. And such is the paradox of living, this ecstasy comes when one is most alive, and it comes as a complete forgetfulness that one is alive. This ecstasy, this forgetfulness of living… came to Buck, leading the pack, sounding the old wolf cry,
20 straining after the food that was alive and that fled swiftly before him through the moonlight… He was mastered by the sheer surging of life, the tidal wave of being, the perfect joy of each separate muscle, joint, and sinew and that it was everything that was not death, that it was aglow and rampant, expressing itself in movement, flying exultantly
25 under the stars and over the face of dead matter that did not move.

But Spitz, cold and calculating even in his supreme moods, left the pack and cut across a narrow piece of land where the creek made a long bend around. Buck did not know this, and as he rounded the bend, the frost wraith of a rabbit still flitting before him, he saw
30 another and larger frost wraith[1] leap from the overhanging bank into the immediate path of the rabbit. It was Spitz.

In a flash Buck knew it. The time had come. It was to the death. As they circled about, snarling, ears laid back, keenly watchful for the advantage, the scene came to Buck with a sense of familiarity.
35 He seemed to remember it all – the white woods, and earth, and moonlight, and the thrill of battle. Over the whiteness and silence brooded a ghostly calm. There was not the faintest whisper of air – nothing moved, not a leaf quivered, the visible breaths of the dogs rising slowly and lingering in the frosty air.

Jack London

Questions

1 What is the 'Tahkeena' (line 1)? Give evidence for how you know this. (2)
2 In the first two paragraphs, what are the dogs chasing? (1)
3 What language technique is used in the phrase 'the tidal wave of being' (line 22)? (1)
4 What is the definition of 'exultantly' (line 24)? (1)

1 A barely visible, ghostly outline.

Punctuation tip: parentheses

Parentheses can be created with commas, dashes or brackets. Just look at these examples:

Buck, a dog with a brown furry coat, raced up the rocky path to the top of the hill.

Buck – a dog with a brown furry coat – raced up the rocky path to the top of the hill.

Buck (a dog with a brown furry coat) raced up the rocky path to the top of the hill.

Rewrite any examples of parentheses you find in the extract from *The Call of the Wild* in a list. How many can you find?

Research

Investigate Buck's way of life, using these questions to guide your research:

● What is a gold rush?
● What places were associated with gold rushes in the nineteenth century?
● What effects did gold rushes have on humans and the natural world?

Talking point

Humans affect the lives of animals in numerous ways, both positively and negatively. In small groups, discuss how humans affect the categories of animals below. You may want to do some research before your discussion to find specific examples.

● Household pets
● Working animals – on farms, in the arctic, in the desert
● Sea creatures and marine life
● Birds
● Wild animals
● Animals in zoos

Writing questions on *Floodland*

1 How would you describe the mood in lines 44–50 and why? (2)
2 What effect does the direct speech have in this passage? (2)
3 Considering the whole passage, what are your impressions of Zoe? (4)

Writing questions on *The Call of the Wild*

1 What is the weather like and how do you know? (2)
2 The rabbit is described as 'like some pale frost wraith' in line 10. Why is this a powerful description? (5)
3 In the final paragraph, how has the writer created an effective atmosphere? (4)

Speaking and listening focus
Debates

Debates often occur over controversial topics, which can mean they get quite heated! It is worth hearing other people's points of view so that you can argue back well. Keeping your cool and listening carefully is the key to successful debating.

You will debate the following statement:

Climate change has nothing to do with children and teenagers.

- Split into small teams and use your research skills to develop fact-based points for one side of the argument. Aim for four points.
- While you're researching, consider the points the other team might be compiling. That way you can work on your **counter-arguments** ahead of the debate.
- When you start debating, remember to stay calm and polite, keeping your points clear and to the point.
- Make sure you acknowledge other people's points and make direct arguments against them. That means listening carefully to what the other team says rather than worrying about your next point.

Thematic focus

An atmosphere of danger runs through both extracts. In one it stems from a natural man-made disaster, in the other from natural animal instincts. Collect quotes from the extracts which show these dangers to add to the examples in the mind map below. Don't forget to use those quotation marks!

Danger → 'Zoe turned and saw with horror'

Once you have collected the quotations, categorise them into natural or man-made dangers. What do you notice?

Extended writing questions

You will now be writing an extended answer about an extract. Write your answer in three PEEA paragraphs, using evidence from the text to support your ideas. (See page 179 in the Exam skills chapter for an explanation of the PEEA technique.)

Here are some tips for writing extended answers:

- Read the questions carefully.
- Use the three foci in your topic sentences for the three paragraphs.
- It might help you to find your evidence for each before you start writing.
- Use connectives like 'and', 'furthermore', 'however' and 'additionally' to expand your explanations.

1 How is a sense of desperation created in Extract 1?

Focus on dialogue, description and structure.

OR

2 How does the author show Buck's natural instincts in Extract 2?

Focus on use of language, vocabulary and structure.

OR

3 Write Zoe's diary entry about this day from Extract 1. You should explore:
- her feelings about the incident with the boats
- how she felt when she woke up after fainting
- what she plans to do now.

Language focus
Voice

Voice is the individual writing style that a writer uses. All the little things, like **syntax**, **tone**, **rhythm** and **vocabulary** make up each person's unique writing style and create a distinctive voice. Our voices are different when we speak so it makes sense that they are different when we write!

Write a descriptive sentence about eating a bar of chocolate. Compare your sentence with someone else's. They're bound to be somewhat different because we all have different voices (and feelings about eating chocolate).

'The Newcomer'

'There's something new in the river,'
The fish said as it swam.
'It's got no scales, no fins, no gills,[1]
And ignores the impassable dam.'

'There's something new[2] in the trees,'
I heard a bloated thrush sing.
'It's got no beak, no claws, no feathers,
And not even the ghost[3] of a wing.'

'There's something new in the warren,'
Said the rabbit to the doe.
'It's got no fur, no eyes, no paws,
Yet digs further than we dare go.'

'There's something new in the whiteness,'
Said the snow-bright polar bear.
'I saw its shadow[4] on a glacier,
But it left no pawmarks there.'

Through the animal kingdom
The news was spreading fast.
No[5] beak, no claws, no feathers,
No scales, no fur, no gills,
It lives in the trees and the water,
In the soil and the snow and the hills,
And it[6] kills and it kills and it kills.[7]

Brian Patten

1. The power of three creates a strong rhythm. Find examples of this technique in other stanzas and decide what each suggests about the different voices.

2. Repetition of 'There's something new…' creates a strong rhythm and because all the animals say it, they have a unified voice.

3. The connotations of 'ghost' are death, danger and otherworldly.

4. What are the connotations of 'shadow'?

5. Repetition of 'no' in the power of three but it is everywhere.

7. This stanza is different from the others. Discuss why you think that might be.

6. The repeated use of 'it' leaves the identity of the Newcomer ambiguous.

33

About the author

Simon Armitage is the UK Poet Laureate. Growing up in Yorkshire, he wrote his first poem aged 10 as a school assignment. He is known for his lively, modern, witty poetry. Armitage wrote 'Ark' for the naming ceremony of the British Antarctic Survey's new ship *RRS Sir David Attenborough* in 2019.

'Ark'

They sent out a dove: it wobbled home,
wings slicked in a rainbow of oil,
a sprig of tinsel snagged in its beak,
a yard of fishing-line binding its feet.

5   *Bring back, bring back the leaf.*

They sent out an arctic fox:
it plodded the bays
of the northern fringe
in muddy socks
10   and a nylon cape.

Bring back, bring back the leaf.
Bring back the reed and the reef,
set the ice sheet back on its frozen plinth,
tuck the restless watercourse into its bed,
15   *sit the glacier down on its highland throne,*
put the snow cap back on the mountain peak.

Let the northern lights be the northern lights
not the alien glow over Glasgow or Leeds.

A camel capsized in a tropical flood.
20   Caimans dozed in Antarctic lakes.
Polymers rolled in the sturgeon's blood.
Hippos wandered the housing estates.

Bring back, bring back the leaf.
Bring back the tusk and the horn
25   *unshorn.*
Bring back the fern, the fish, the frond and the fowl,
the golden toad and the pygmy owl,
revisit the scene
where swallowtails fly
30   *through acres of unexhausted sky.*

They sent out a boat.
Go little breaker,
splinter the pack-ice and floes, nose
through the rafts and pads
35   of wrappers and bottles and nurdles and cans,
the bergs and atolls and islands and states
of plastic bags and micro-beads
and the forests of smoke.

Bring back, bring back the leaf,
40   *bring back the river and sea.*

Simon Armitage

Questions

1 What is the definition of 'restless' (line 14)? (1)
2 What language technique is used in 'camel capsized' (line 19)? (1)
3 Where are the hippos? (1)
  a in a river
  b at a supermarket
  c under a waterfall
  d on a housing estate
4 What is the 'alien glow over Glasgow or Leeds' (line 18)? (1) **FP**
5 Name one thing the boat encounters in the penultimate stanza. (1)

Text features

Song or poem?

Look again at the poem. Don't read it, just look at it. What do you notice? You are looking at the **shape** and structure of the poem.

In 'Ark', the parts in italic really stick out when we look at it. It looks like song lyrics. It's the shape of a song. The parts in italic are the chorus and the other stanzas are the verses.

The fact, that Armitage repeats the **refrain** 'bring back, bring back the leaf' also reminds us of a song, even though it varies in length and the tone becomes plaintive when it is longer. Patten also uses repetition in 'The Newcomer' in 'There's something new', which feels like a repetitive, insistent beat. They're like catchy protest songs that you can't get out of your head.

It could be argued that songs and poems are one and the same; for example, they both have rhythm, sometimes **rhyme**. But why do you think Armitage and Patten use this song-like structure and tone for this topic?

Language focus

Irony

Irony sounds complicated but it is straightforward (ironically!). Irony is the use of words to convey the opposite to their actual meaning or to what is expected. You must be alert to irony, otherwise you will miss the writer's real meaning. Here are some different types of irony:

1 **Verbal irony** can involve humour, but not always. Sarcasm can be confused with irony, but being sarcastic is more deliberately mean. For example, a 'rainbow of oil' is a beautiful description but the contrast of a multicoloured rainbow and the oil covering the bird is completely oppositional.

2 **Situational irony** is when something happens which is the opposite of the expectation; for example, a fire station burning down or a camel capsizing in a flood.

3 **Dramatic irony** occurs when the audience or reader knows something that the characters do not. In the case of 'The Newcomer', the animals do not know what the 'something new' is but the reader does.

Come up with three examples of each type of irony from books or films you've read or seen.

Writing questions on *Ark*

1 How is the description of the dove effective? (4)

2 What is the fox wearing and why is it significant? (2)

3 What do you think is effective about the structure of this poem? (4)

4 Why do you think the poem is called 'Ark'? (2)

5 What similarities have you noticed between 'Ark' and 'The Newcomer'? Explain your observations using evidence from both poems to support your points. (4)

About the author

Adrienne Matei, a Canadian journalist, comments in this article on a report that 'revealed that a mind-boggling 13.3 quadrillion microfibers (infinitesimal strands of fabric) were released into the California environment in 2019'.

'Your polyester sweater is destroying the environment. Here's why'

Boycotting polyester would reduce microfiber pollution. But the larger problem is the sheer volume of clothing we buy and discard.

All fabrics release microfibers, whether they are organic, like hemp and wool, or synthetic, like polyester and acrylic. Since their discovery in
5 2011 by ecologist Mark Browne, much of the conversation surrounding microfibers has focused on synthetic fibers in particular. That's because, as a product of the petrochemical industry, synthetic fabric is essentially plastic, making the microfibers it releases a form of microplastic pollution. Plastic microfibers are a disturbingly abundant
10 foreign substance in the Earth's ecosystem – they make up 90% of the microplastic pollution in the Atlantic Ocean, and are easily ingested by the tiny fish and plankton that support the entire marine ecosystem.

While larger pieces of plastic garbage in the ocean are largely attributed to poor waste management in rapidly developing economies, microfiber
15 pollution is predominantly linked to wastewater from developed nations, according to an article recently published by the American Association of Textile Chemists and Colorists. Clothing releases the most microfibers while being machine-washed, and many of those fibers elude filtration in treatment centres, ultimately ending up in waterways
20 and oceans. One study from 2017 even found that 83% of global tap water samples contained microfibers.

So, is the solution to stop buying synthetic clothing?

'Shifting away from synthetic fabrics is one way to reduce microplastics in the ocean,' says Dr Brian Hunt, a biological oceanographer at the
25 University of British Columbia. 'Decreasing the demand for synthetics would decrease production.'

Recently, some retailers have marketed 'anti-microbial' or 'anti-odour' clothing they claim requires only infrequent washing; Hunt considers such initiatives, as well as a movement among eco-conscious consumers
30 to buy more organic, natural fabrics, generally encouraging.

'But still,' he says, 'there's the question of: what happens with these new approaches? Everything we do has some kind of effect. Even with natural clothing, depending on how it's treated, there might be some contributions to pollution in the ocean.'

35 Wool and cotton may be chemically processed; they also require much water and energy to produce. Buying lots of fancy new environmentally friendly gear is still less sustainable than sticking with what you already have. In the same sense, boycotting polyester is good, but let's not forget the problem of microfibers is amplified by the amount of clothing we're
40 producing and buying on a macro level.

The emergence of fast fashion in the early 2000s introduced consumers to cheaply made, often synthetic clothing on a massive scale. A growing middle class has helped clothing production double in the last 15 years, according to the Ellen McArthur Foundation, an environmental charity;
45 the global clothing industry is estimated to grow from $1.9tn in 2019 to over $3tn by 2030. Textile production is the world's second-most polluting industry, behind only oil – and every year we prematurely discard $400bn worth of clothing.

Fashion corporations must be held accountable for implementing
50 sustainable practices across their supply chains, including developing and using sustainable fabrics that do not emit microplastics. On a consumer level, we need to ensure the trend of resale continues its encouraging trajectory by shopping thrift and vintage, renting trendy and special occasion-wear, and consigning or donating our used clothing. We can
55 also wash our clothing less frequently and in cold, quick cycles – this reduces microfiber shedding, and helps retain the clothes' quality, too.

Did you know that you can often recycle old clothing almost the same way you recycle bottles and cans? In many places you can bring old clothes to specific textile recycling depots or sign up for a free recycling
60 program. In 2018, a Hong Kong textile mill even pioneered a technology which recycles waste textiles into new yarn on an unprecedented scale. The technology caught the interest of fast-fashion giants...

With effort and innovation, microfiber pollution – among the other environmental ills caused by the fashion industry at large – can be
65 reduced. As for the quadrillions of fibers the fabrics all around you are shedding: think of them the next time you catch yourself impulse shopping for a new outfit, and perhaps take a minute to reflect on whether you have enough, already.

Adrienne Matei
(Source: *Guardian* online, 20 October 2020)

Questions

1 What is the definition of 'abundant'? (1)
2 What percentage of microplastic pollution in the Atlantic Ocean is made up of microfibers? (1)
3 What is the 'world's second-most polluting industry'? (1)
4 Identify one example of a rhetorical question in the article and explain its effect. (2)
5 Using your own words, summarise the two solutions the writer offers to the problem in the last paragraph. (2)
6 Looking at the extract as a whole, in what ways does the information the writer provides make the message all the more powerful? (4)

Text features
Structuring and engaging

This article is full of facts and opinions but does not feel overwhelming because it's well-organised. As writers, you can use the following structural features to help organise your own persuasive and discursive writing pieces:

- **Rhetorical questions** – asking a question that the reader might be wondering and then answering it can act like a subheading.
- **Subheadings** – giving each paragraph or section a subheading helps the reader keep track of the different areas the writer covers.
- **Bullet points** – lists are useful to summarise ideas or itemise points but writing them all in a long sentence can be confusing. Break them up with bullet points.
- **Linking words and phrases** – words/phrases like 'however', 'in many cases', 'also' and 'but' act like signposts, guiding a reader through the different ideas, whether they compare or contrast.

Language focus

A strong ending

The article is opinion-based but still informative and discursive. It becomes more persuasive in the conclusion, where we are offered solutions to the problem, which means we are left with a clear understanding of the writer's viewpoint. These techniques will help make your conclusions stronger:

- the power of three
- a rhetorical question, for example: *How many more tons of waste will we create?*
- a short impact statement to create a strong ending too, for example: *We must recycle to save the seas.*
- a call to action, for example: *think of them [all the microfibers] the next time you catch yourself impulse shopping for a new outfit.*

On the other hand

Counter-arguments are important in persuasive and discursive writing. In persuasive writing you want to quash them, but in discursive you must acknowledge them (even if you don't agree with them).

Think of some counter-arguments for the points in the article, for example: *While new textile production is a great idea, it will take time to reinvent fabrics and this problem needs to be solved quickly.*

 # Drama focus

Characterful creatures

In small groups, perform a conversation between different animals on this topic. Ensure each animal character has a unique voice, expression and physicality. Switching parts halfway through will reveal how different people play the same animal.

Writing task

You are going to write a persuasive article called 'Why we must recycle plastic'. You can use facts and statistics from the extract or research your own.

Writing persuasively

Give yourself five minutes to write down all the ideas and relevant points you can think of. Pick your best three. These might be ideas that you think you can expand on, know the most about or you just feel they're the strongest persuasively. These three ideas will become your three **topic sentences** which will start each of your main paragraphs.

Think of your structure as a sandwich. The introduction and conclusion are the bread but within them you have layers of different fillings, the topic sentences being the best and juiciest bits!

To garnish, pepper with persuasive language techniques, such as rhetorical questions, repetition and collective nouns (see page 172 in Loud and proud for a checklist of techniques).

Use this structure to help plan your work:

Title: Why we must recycle more plastic

Introduction

What is your article about? Be brief, give a background to what you are writing about, why it is important and make it clear what your point of view is.

Paragraph 1

First point and evidence. Choose your strongest point for this.

Paragraph 2

Second point and evidence. Acknowledge a possible counter-argument to your reason and quash it!

Paragraph 3

Third point and evidence.

Conclusion

Aim for three sentences. Summarise your argument, possibly using the power of three. Give your own opinion again and finish with a short, impactful statement or rhetorical question.

Time to write

Now it's time to write up your finished article. Aim for three main body paragraphs, as planned above.

Write a persuasive article with the title: 'Why we must recycle plastic'.

Putting pen to paper

Now try one of the writing tasks below. You may want to do some of your own research before starting your piece.

1 'Children should be leading the way in climate action.' Write a discursive essay using this statement as a starting point.
2 'The beauty of the planet outweighs our need for fuel.' Use this as the first line of a persuasive argument.
3 'Veganism is the best solution to saving our planet.' Decide whether you agree or disagree with this statement and write an essay from one side of the argument.

Peer review (editing/drafting)

Reviewing your writing

Swap your writing with a partner. Read each other's work carefully, looking at:

- topic sentences – are they at the start of each paragraph?
- the way ideas/points of view are expressed – are they clear?
- how the article is structured – do the ideas link well?

Find two positive things that would improve the writing in your view. Share these with your partner.

Edit your work, considering these changes and correcting any spelling or punctuation errors.

Wider reading

If you want to read more about protecting our planet, have a look at these brilliant books:

- *No One is Too Small to Make a Difference* by Greta Thunberg
- *Breathe* by Sarah Crossan
- *Born Free* by Joy Adamson*
- *Beetle Boy* by MG Leonard
- *Collected Poems for Children* by Ted Hughes*
- *My Family and Other Animals* by Gerald Durrell
- 'Q&A: Christmas Lecturer talks geoscience' by Chris Jackson – search at: www.imperial.ac.uk
- *Watership Down* by Richard Adams*

*Choose these titles for a more challenging read!

Book review

Prepare interview questions for a character from a book you have read recently. It might be one from the wider reading list above.

Ask a partner to ask you the questions as the character. What do they think of the character? Does it make them want to read the book?

3 Technology and communication

Aims

- **Reading focus**: Tone and mood
- **Writing focus**: Discursive article
- **Speaking and listening focus**: Developing arguments
- **Language focus**: Imagery, narrative perspective and statistics, paragraphing
- **Drama focus**: Costume design

Context

The way we communicate has changed irrevocably in the last decade. During the global Coronavirus pandemic and with people becoming more climate change-aware over travel, technology has become the overarching method of communicating with family, friends, work and school colleagues.

In this chapter, we will read how classic science-fiction and dystopian novels have cast technology in a dangerous light but in recent drama and non-fiction, writers are portraying it as a force for good and even to generate humour. You will then get to weigh up the advantages and disadvantages of the way teenagers use technology and communicate with others in a discursive article.

About the author

Isaac Asimov (1920–1992) was an American science-fiction writer. His *I, Robot* was first published in scientific magazines between 1940 and 1950. The three short stories explored how robots could interact with humans without conflict or mistrust. As well as being a writer, Asimov was a biochemistry professor at Boston University.

In this extract, we met Robbie, a robot companion of a young human, Gloria. Even after two years of excellent care by Robbie, Gloria's mother is still uncertain about her daughter's closeness to the robot.

I, Robot

'Ninety-eight–ninety-nine–one hundred.' Gloria withdrew her chubby little forearm from before her eyes and stood for a moment, wrinkling her nose and blinking in the sunlight. Then, trying to watch in all directions at once, she withdrew a few cautious steps from the tree
5 against which she had been leaning.

She craned her neck to investigate the possibilities of a clump of bushes to the right and then withdrew farther to obtain a better angle for viewing its dark recesses. The quiet was profound except for the incessant buzzing of insects and the occasional chirrup of some hardy
10 bird, braving the midday sun.

Gloria pouted, 'I bet he went inside the house, and I've told him a million times that that's not fair.'

With tiny lips pressed together tightly and a severe frown crinkling her forehead, she moved determinedly toward the two-story building up
15 past the driveway.

Too late she heard the rustling sound behind her, followed by the distinctive and rhythmic clump-clump of Robbie's metal feet. She whirled about to see her triumphing companion emerge from hiding and make for the home-tree at full speed.

20 Gloria shrieked in dismay. 'Wait, Robbie! That wasn't fair, Robbie! You promised you wouldn't run until I found you.' Her little feet could make no headway at all against Robbie's giant strides. Then, within ten feet of the goal, Robbie's pace slowed suddenly to the merest of crawls, and Gloria, with one final burst of wild speed, dashed pantingly past
25 him to touch the welcome bark of home-tree first.

Gleefully, she turned on the faithful Robbie, and with the basest of ingratitude, rewarded him for his sacrifice by taunting him cruelly for a lack of running ability.

'Robbie can't run,' she shouted at the top of her eight-year-old voice.
30 'I can beat him any day. I can beat him any day.' She chanted the words in a shrill rhythm.

Robbie didn't answer, of course – not in words. He pantomimed running instead, inching away until Gloria found herself running after him as he dodged her narrowly, forcing her to veer in helpless circles,
35 little arms outstretched and fanning at the air.

'Robbie,' she squealed, 'stand still!' – And the laughter was forced out of her in breathless jerks. –

Until he turned suddenly and caught her up, whirling her round, so that for her the world fell away for a moment with a blue emptiness
40 beneath, and green trees stretching hungrily downward toward the void. Then she was down in the grass again, leaning against Robbie's leg and still holding a hard, metal finger.

After a while, her breath returned. She pushed uselessly at her dishevelled hair in vague imitation of one of her mother's gestures and
45 twisted to see if her dress were torn.

She slapped her hand against Robbie's torso, 'Bad boy! […] But anyway, it's my turn to hide now because you've got longer legs and you promised not to run till I found you.'

> **1** A three-dimensional form of which each face is a parallelogram.

Robbie nodded his head – a small parallelepiped[1] with rounded edges
50 and corners attached to a similar but much larger parallelepiped that served as torso by means of a short, flexible stalk – and obediently faced the tree. A thin, metal film descended over his glowing eyes and from within his body came a steady, resonant ticking.

'Don't peek now – and don't skip any numbers,' warned Gloria, and
55 scurried for cover.

With unvarying regularity, seconds were ticked off, and at the hundredth, up went the eyelids, and the glowing red of Robbie's eyes swept the prospect. They rested for a moment on a bit of colourful

> **2** A type of cotton cloth patterned with coloured squares on a white background.

gingham[2] that protruded from behind a boulder. He advanced a few
60 steps and convinced himself that it was Gloria who squatted behind it.

Slowly, remaining always between Gloria and home-tree, he advanced on the hiding place, and when Gloria was plainly in sight and could no longer even theorise to herself that she was not seen, he extended one arm toward her, slapping the other against his leg so that it rang again.
65 Gloria emerged sulkily.

Isaac Asimov

Questions

1 Find a phrase that tells you what the weather is like. (1)
2 In the context of the passage, what does 'pouted' mean (line 11)? (1)
3 What language technique is used in 'green trees stretching hungrily' (line 40)? (1)
4 Read lines 58–60. In your own words, explain how Robbie spots Gloria. (1)
5 What game are Robbie and Gloria playing? (1)
   a 'it'
   b hide and seek
   c hopscotch
   d football

Read more

Asimov wrote a variety of non-fiction and fiction that you might like to discover yourself. If you like art or illustration, however, look out for *The Wild Robot* by writer and illustrator, Peter Brown. When robot Roz opens her eyes for the first time, she finds herself alone on a remote island. Can she survive the wilderness?

Punctuation focus
Signalling paragraphs

Knowing when to start a new paragraph in the flow of writing can be tricky. Remember, you can always go back during proofreading and add // where you would have liked a new paragraph to start. Or try this **TiP-ToP** technique to get it right in the first place.

Start a new paragraph when one of these changes:

- **Ti**me, for example: *Later that night...*
- **P**lace, for example: *We got to the park just as the sun was setting...*
- **To**pic, for example: *On the other hand, foxes are also gentle creatures...*
- **P**erson, for example: *'Get back to your lesson, Maude!' Ms Miller shouted. In response, Maude hollered, 'You couldn't pay me to come back to Maths!'*

Read back through the extract from *I, Robot* and label each new paragraph with the reason why the paragraph has changed. Time, place, topic or person?

About the author

Ray Bradbury (1920–2012) was an American author and screenwriter. Bradbury was hugely influenced by poetry and drama, as well as magic – he had dreamt of being a magician at one point.

Bradbury is probably best known for his dystopian novel *Fahrenheit 451* (1953). In this future society where technology and media have taken over, books are outlawed and are burned if discovered. Firemen don't stop fires, they start them. One such fireman, Guy Montag, is becoming disillusioned with his job so when the opportunity arises on a book-burning job, he takes the chance to see for himself what a banned book can offer.

Fahrenheit 451

Books bombarded his shoulders, his arms, his upturned face. A book alighted, almost obediently, like a white pigeon, in his hands, wings fluttering. In the dim, wavering light, a page hung open and it was like a snowy white feather, the words delicately painted thereon. In all
5 the rush and fervour Montag had only an instant to read a line, but it blazed in his mind for the next minute as if stamped there with fiery steel. 'Time has fallen asleep in the afternoon sunshine.' He dropped the book. Immediately, another fell into his arms.

'Montag, up here!'

10 Montag's hand closed like a mouth, crushed the book with wild devotion with an insanity of mindlessness to his chest. The men above were hurling shovelfuls of magazines into the dusty air. They fell like slaughtered birds and the woman stood below, like a small girl among the bodies.

Montag had done nothing. His hand had done it all, his hand, with a
15 brain of its own, with a conscience and a curiosity in each trembling finger, had turned thief. Now, it plunged the book back under his arm, pressed it tight to sweating armpit, rushed out empty, with a magician's flourish! Look here! Innocent! Look!

He gazed, shaken, at that white hand. He held it way out, as if he were
20 far-sighted. He held it close, as if he were blind.

'Montag!'

He jerked about.

'Don't stand there, idiot!'

The books lay like great mounds of fishes left to dry. The men danced and
25 slipped and fell over them. Titles glittered their golden eyes, falling, gone.

1 A combustible liquid, also known as paraffin.

2 A biblical reference to a city in which God created multiple languages to punish the humans living there so they could not understand each other.

'Kerosene!'[1]

They pumped the cold fluid from the numbered 451 tanks strapped to their
30 shoulders. They coated each book, they pumped rooms full of it.

They hurried downstairs, Montag staggered after them
35 in the kerosene fumes.

'Come on, woman!'

The woman knelt among the books, touching the drenched leather and cardboard, reading the gilt titles with her fingers while her eyes accused Montag.

40 'You can't have my books,' she said.

'You know the law,' said Beatty. 'Where's your common sense? None of these books agree with each other. You've been locked up here for years with a regular damned Tower of Babel[2]. Snap out of it! The people in those books never lived. Come on now!'

45 She shook her head.

'The whole house is going up,' said Beatty.

The men walked clumsily to the door. They glanced back at Montag, who stood near the woman.

'You're not leaving her here?' he protested.

50 'She won't come.'

'Force her then!'

Beatty raised his hand in which was concealed the igniter. 'We're due back at the house. Besides, these fanatics always try suicide; the pattern's familiar.'

55 Montag placed his hand on the woman's elbow. 'You can come with me.'

'No,' she said. 'Thank you, anyway.'

Ray Bradbury

Questions

1 What is the definition of 'fervour' (line 5)? (1)
2 Montag reads a line from the book in the first paragraph of the extract. True or false? (1) FP
3 Identify the two language techniques used in 'Titles glittered their golden eyes' (line 25). (2)
4 Choose an adjective that describes Beatty. (1)

Research

Take some time to research this post-war period using the following topics:

- the birth of the teenager
- 1950s television or pop music
- McCarthyism and its effects
- the Cold War.

Talking point

In pairs, make a list of how humans have communicated through the ages. Reach as far back as you can! Once you think you've completed the list, share it with another pair. Discuss the benefits and drawbacks of each communication method.

Finally, consider whether technology has impacted communication positively or negatively. Share your final thoughts with the whole class.

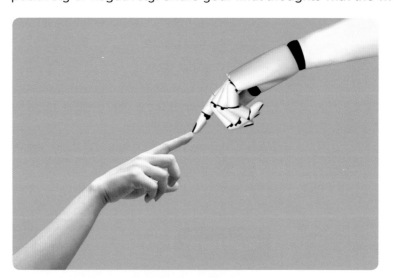

Punctuation tip

Finish what you've started. Double check you have started your sentence with a capital letter and finished it with a full stop or another appropriate punctuation mark. It's easy to miss these if you rush to complete work or get distracted.

Writing questions on _I, Robot_

1 Robbie is a robot. Find two quotations and explain how the writer suggests this. (4)
2 What do Robbie's reactions to Gloria and the game suggest about him? (4)
3 Does Gloria enjoy her time with Robbie? Refer closely to the text in your answer. (3)

Writing questions on *Fahrenheit 451*

1   The author uses several similes in lines 1–13. Choose two and discuss their effect. (4)
2   What is your impression of Guy Montag? (4)
3   How is tension created throughout the passage? (6)

Speaking and listening focus
Spoken argument

Developing a spoken argument is vital in many circumstances. Learning to do this briefly and articulately is key and using signpost words or phrases can be a great help. These are sometimes called **discourse markers**.

In small groups, discuss the pros and cons of using a virtual assistant at home. Everyone should have three points prepared but they can jump in and develop other people's points too. Each point that is made must include one of the following discourse markers:

> *firstly   conversely   similarly   on the other hand   furthermore more importantly   in conclusion   despite that   equally   in addition whereas   however*

Look back at page 31 in Our planet for some tips on how to keep your debate focused.

This exercise will be helpful for the writing task later in this chapter when you could draft your points verbally with a partner.

Thematic focus

The **tone** of a piece of writing is the feeling or atmosphere created by the writer. **Mood** is the feeling or atmosphere a reader feels as they read the piece of writing. They are very similar, but they are different. Here are some examples:

Tone	Mood
angry	gloomy
suspicious	tense
cheerful	enraged
playful	intrigued
sympathetic	inspired
witty	hopeful

Choose a tone and choose a mood that is created by the Asimov and Bradbury extracts from the list above or one you've thought of yourself. Then find words from each extract which suggest that tone and mood. One example has been started for you below:

Extract 1: Asimov		Extract 2: Bradbury	
Tone chosen:	Mood chosen: *Intrigued*	Tone chosen:	Mood chosen:
	glowing *resonant*		

Extended writing questions

You will now be writing an extended answer about an extract. Write your answer in three PEEA paragraphs, using evidence from the text to support your ideas. (See page 179 in the Exam skills chapter for an explanation of the PEEA technique.)

Here are some tips for writing extended answers:

- Read the questions carefully.
- Use the three foci in your topic sentences for the three paragraphs.
- It might help you to find your evidence for each before you start writing.
- Use connectives like 'and', 'furthermore', 'however' and 'additionally' to expand your explanations.

1 In Extract 1 from *I, Robot*, how does the author show that robots and humans could live together peacefully?

   Consider vocabulary, character description and tone in your answer to this question.

OR

2 In Extract 2 from *Fahrenheit 451*, how does the author create a sense of contrast between the regime Montag is living under and what it is trying to destroy?

   Refer to imagery, vocabulary and sentence construction in your answer to this question.

OR

3 Write a conversation between Gloria and one of her friends explaining her relationship with Robbie in *I, Robot*.

   You should explore how Robbie reacts to her, how they communicate and her feelings towards Robbie.

Punctuation tip

Do you always need a comma before 'but'? If you are joining two independent clauses, then you can place a comma before the conjunction.

For example: *We eventually found our seats + Zoe was not there = We eventually found our seats, but Zoe was not there.*

About the author

Ian McWethy is an American actor, screenwriter and playwright. He has written over 40 one-act plays and is currently working on adaptations of his plays for online productions.

In this extract from *The Internet is Distract–OH LOOK A KITTEN!* (2015), Micah has an essay to finish about *The Great Gatsby* but her best friend, Taylor, is constantly checking up on her when she needs to do some research, and she keeps getting distracted by pesky cat videos.

The Internet is Distract–OH LOOK A KITTEN!

MICAH Alright, three more sentences. Here we go.

(MICAH takes a deep breath and starts typing)

MICAH *(Typing whilst talking:)* In the end, Jay Gatsby never did get what he wanted, his precious and elusive…light. *(Stops to think.)* Shoot,
5 what colour was that light? Blue? The book cover's blue. *(Typing:)* His precious and elusive blue light. *(Thinking:)* It's not blue. Darn it. It's… it's…Wifi on!

(MICAH turns back on the internet browser.

Lights up stage left where GOOGLE appears)

10 GOOGLE Hi. Welcome to Google, where we have everything you want forever. Would you like a search engine? Email? Calendar? Cloud computing? A terrible social media platform no one uses?

MICAH Wikipedia.

GOOGLE Wikipedia, wonderful. Coming right up!

15 *(Lights out on GOOGLE.*

Lights up on stage right where WIKIPEDIA is waiting for MICAH.)

WIKIPEDIA Hi, welcome to Wikipedia, a –

(TAYLOR's light comes back on stage left.)

TAYLOR *(Interrupting:)* Hey, you're back. Did you finish your essay?

20 MICAH No, not yet. I forgot what colour the light was in *The Great Gatsby*.

TAYLOR What light?

MICAH The…light. The light that haunts Jay Gatsby. Daisy's light.

TAYLOR I don't remember there being a light. But I skipped through
25 a lot of it. It was really long.

MICAH It's 180 pages.

TAYLOR Yeah, but anything over 140 characters, unless it has emojis is kinds hard for me to follow these days.

MICAH Well, look, there's definitely a light in *The Great Gatsby*, and I
30 know Mr Fishbine will knock points off if I get its colour wrong so…

TAYLOR Oh! Hey, have you seen The Great Catsby? Open YouTube!

(Lights up on CAT, who's now dressed as Nick Carraway[1])

1 Nick Carraway is the narrator of *The Great Gatsby*.

CATSBY New York. 1922. The tempo of the city had changed sharply. The buildings were higher. The parties were bigger. The morals were
35 looser. And the liquor was cheaper.

MICAH No! No more cat videos! I have to work. Close window.

(Lights out on CATSBY)

TAYLOR That cat just recited *The Great Gatsby* in perfect English. How are you not impressed by that!?!

40 MICAH Taylor, I really have to finish this.

TAYLOR Fine. Just chat me again when you're done.

MICAH Close window!

(Lights out on TAYLOR)

MICAH Maximise Wikipedia!

45 *(Lights back up on WIKIPEDIA)*

WIKIPEDIA Hi, welcome to Wikipedia, a collaboratively edited, multilingual, free-access, free content internet encyclopaedia. Wikipedia is a mostly reliable resource.

MICAH Yeah, what colour is the light in *The Great Gatsby*?

50 WIKIPEDIA Hmmm…Not found. Contents for *The Great Gatsby*. 1.1. Historical context 2. Plot summary 2.1 Major characters 3. Themes.

MICAH Never mind, this will take too long. Search for: Light.

WIKIPEDIA *(Skipping down the article:)*…Gatsby spends many nights
55 staring at the green light at the end of her dock, across the bay from his mansion. The colour of the light is green dur to Daisy's romantic attraction to Kermit the Frog, of The Muppets and Sesame Street Fame. In chapter five she insists –

MICAH Green! Okay, that's all I needed. Thanks! That's right. Wifi O –
60 Wait. Kermit the Frog? What was that? Kermit the Frog wasn't in *The Great Gatsby*!

WIKIPEDIA Uh-oh! Looks like you've found a Woopsipedia!

Ian McWethy

51

Text features
Character perspective

The characters in this drama script are unusual. The playwright has personified websites and made the **archetypal** cat video a character in itself! Personification is being used to make this script engaging and amusing. We are used to having narrators telling the story but not websites!

Micah's is, however, the main narrative perspective. It's as if we're seeing the events through her eyes. The same is true for the extract from *Fahrenheit 451* – we see the action from Montag's point of view, even though it is written in **third person**.

A good way of thinking about perspective is imagining how the text would be filmed. Which character would the camera focus on or from whose point of view would the events unfold on the screen? That's usually whose perspective it's written from.

Language focus
Stage directions

Stage directions in a script are usually in brackets or italics. You do not read these aloud; they are just to guide the director or actor. Ian McWethy gives instructions about the lighting to bring the scene to life and make it more humorous.

The lighting changes are abrupt and move quickly between the different characters. This emphasises how Micah is getting distracted by her friend and by flicking between windows on her computer. Punctuation also reveals this in the script itself. Playwrights show when a character is interrupted by an incomplete sentence followed by a dash. For example:

In chapter five she insists –

When reading the script aloud, you would need to read the next line quickly to show this interruption.

About the author

Sabrina Barr is Lifestyle Writer for *The Independent*. She enjoys writing about feminism, body positivity, social issues, wellbeing, relationships and current trends.

Lockdown refers to the period in 2020–2021 during which the Coronavirus pandemic caused the British government to close non-essential shops, workplaces, schools, restaurants and leisure facilities. The British public stayed at home to minimise the effect the spread of the virus.

'UK adults "spending a quarter of their waking lives online due to lockdown"'

'Lockdown may leave a lasting digital legacy,' Ofcom spokesperson states.

UK adults are spending approximately a quarter of their waking lives online due to the coronavirus
5 lockdown, a study conducted by Ofcom has found.

In Ofcom's latest Online Nation report for April, the broadcast regulator noted that adults across the nation are spending an average of just over four hours a day online.

10 This figure marked an increase from September last year, when it was reported that adults were spending around three and a half hours online on a daily basis.

According to the report, use of platforms such as
15 TikTok and Zoom has significantly contributed to the increase in time spent online during lockdown, which was first established across the UK on 23 March.

Ofcom found that from January to April this year,
20 the number of UK visitors on video-sharing app TikTok rose from 5.4 million to 12.9 million.

Meanwhile, the number of UK users of video-conferencing platform Zoom soared from 659,000 in January to 13 million in April.

25 The report also noted that the number of UK adults making video calls has doubled during lockdown, with 7 in 10 conducting weekly video calls.

Furthermore, the number of adults aged over 65 who make video calls at least once a week has
30 increased from 22 per cent in February to 61 per cent in May.

Yih-Choung Teh, director of strategy and research at Ofcom, described the lasting effect lockdown is likely to have on the way people communicate
35 with each other, as indicated by the report.

'Lockdown may leave a lasting digital legacy,' Teh said.

'Coronavirus has radically changed the way we live, work and communicate online, with millions of
40 people using online video services for the first time.'

The Ofcom spokesperson added that it is essential to ensure that internet users are protected as people spend more time online.

'As the way we communicate evolves and people
45 broaden their online horizons, our role is to help ensure that people have a positive experience, and that they're safe and protected,' Teh stated.

According to the Ofcom study, 87 per cent of adults said they felt concerned about children
50 using video-sharing platforms and other apps.

More than half said they wish to see more efficient regulation on said platforms, a decrease from 64 per cent who said so in 2019.

Sabrina Barr

(Source: *The Independent* online, 24 June 2020)

Questions

1 How much more time were adults spending online in April 2020 compared to September 2019? (1)
2 What is Yih-Choung Teh's job? (1)
3 Read lines 14–24. Why do you think TikTok and Zoom were such popular platforms during lockdown? (4)
4 Summarise what Yih-Choung Teh is quoted as saying. (3)
5 Looking at the whole article, what tone is created and how? Refer to the text closely in your answer. (2)

Text features

Text bias

Biased information is written from a particular perspective or point of view. The internet is full of **bias** – purposefully and accidentally. As a result, the information becomes unreliable. For example, 'I thought the movie was great'.

When a piece of writing is balanced, it offers a variety of different views that give a rounded overview of the issue. For example, 'I thought the movie was great, but my friend did not rate the production quality.'

But there is a third option: neutrality. Neutral means complete objectivity and a detachment from the writer. It is pure fact. For example, 'The movie made $100 billion at the box office'.

Decide whether the article by Sabrina Barr is biased, balanced or neutral.

 # Language focus

Special effects in non-fiction

Don't forget that language techniques can be used in non-fiction writing as well as fiction writing.

Comparing through metaphor, simile or personification can create **hyperbolic** language in order to be more persuasive or help a reader understand and remember your point.

Even the article above does this with an example of alliteration:

***L**ockdown may **l**eave a **l**asting digital **l**egacy.*

The repetition of the 'l' sound stretches out the phrase, implying the length of time.

Sibilance is a form of alliteration that specifically uses 's', 'sh' or 'z' sounds in a group of words. For example:

***S**izzling **s**ausage**s** in a **s**auce**p**an.*

In this case, the repetition of the 's' sounds create the sound of the meat being cooked.

There is more information about alliteration and assonance on page 19 in Growing up.

Drama focus

Imagine you have been asked to design the costumes for the drama extract on page 50. How would Google and Wikipedia be dressed? You may want to create drawings just like a professional designer would do – you could use a digital design programme too. Try to assemble at least part of the costume to perform the script in.

Consider the difference being in costume makes to your reading.

Writing task

Now you have had an insight into adults' technological usage, it's your turn! You are going to write a discursive article about the issues and benefits of teenagers' technology use.

Create a strong start to your article by using this formula (in any order) for a five-sentence introduction:

● an anecdote related to the title (two sentences)
● a rhetorical question
● a simile
● acknowledgement you are looking at both sides of the argument.

Check back to page 38 in the Our planet chapter to learn more about strong endings.

Use the structure below to plan the points and evidence you will use in your article:

Benefits	Issues
Ability to work with people from all around the country and world makes me more open-minded and connected, e.g. with family and friends.	*Isolation from real human connection, e.g. benefit of real contact to understand each other better, such as body language.*

In your article, make sure you select an equal number of ideas from each column. You might not write up all the points you have planned or you might merge a couple together. That's okay! A plan can change, that's the beauty of a plan.

Remember to use signpost words and phrases (discourse markers) to link your ideas together and structure your article. Here are some helpful ones:

> *firstly   on the other hand   furthermore   in conclusion
> in addition   whereas   lastly*

Look back at the Speaking and listening focus on page 47 for some more examples.

Time to write

Write a discursive article about the issues and benefits of teenagers' technology use.

Putting pen to paper

Now try one of the writing tasks below. You may want to do some of your own research before starting your piece.

1   Write a newspaper article exploring the advantages and disadvantages of playing computer games.
2   Write an article for a magazine discussing the potential use of artificial intelligence in schools.
3   'Effective communication only happens face to face.' Discuss both sides of this statement.

Peer review (editing/drafting)

Reviewing your writing

Swap your writing with a partner. Read each other's work carefully, looking at:

● the signpost words and phrases – do they help guide your reading and understanding of the different points and ideas?
● the way ideas/points of view are expressed – are they clear?
● how the article is structured – do the ideas link well?

Find two positive things that would improve the writing in your view. Share these with your partner.

Edit your work, considering these changes and correcting any spelling or punctuation errors.

Wider reading

If you want to read more about technology and communication, have a look at these brilliant books:

● *The Boy Who Made the World Disappear* by Ben Miller
● *Railhead* by Philip Reeve
● *Earthfall* by Mark Walden
● *Hacker* by Malorie Blackman
● *The Giver* by Lois Lowry
● *Uglies* by Scott Westerfield*
● *Code Name Verity* by Elizabeth Wein
● *Gone* by Michael Grant

*Choose these titles for a more challenging read!

Book review

Write a message exchange between two characters from a book about science, technology or futuristic worlds that you have read recently. It might be one from the wider reading list above.

Ask a partner to read the exchange with you, each playing a character. What does your partner think of the characters and their relationship? Does it make them want to read the book?

4 Journeying

Context

Travel opens your mind and broadens your horizons by introducing you to new cultures, people and places. Wherever you go, it changes you. But characters (and real-life people!) do not always go on physical journeys — they can be emotional too. Name any famous character and even if they go on a physical quest, defeating foes and saving the world, they will have learnt something or grown up or developed in the process.

The characters in the extracts that follow all have different reasons for travelling — escape, adventure and a search for knowledge. At the end of your journey through this chapter, you will have produced your own piece of travel writing, describing the atmosphere of a place you have enjoyed visiting.

About the author

Jules Verne (1828–1905) was a French poet, novelist and playwright. He has been the second most translated author in the world between Agatha Christie and William Shakespeare. He is most famous for his three *Voyages Extraordinaires* novels, which include *Around the World in 80 Days* (1872).

Phileas Fogg, a wealthy man living in solitude in London, and his newly employed French valet, Passpartout, set out to circumnavigate the world in 80 days after being challenged by a friend. In this extract, they are near the beginning of their journey, travelling through India on a train.

Around the World in 80 Days

The train had started punctually. Among the passengers were a number of officers, Government officials, and opium and indigo merchants, whose business called them to the eastern coast. Passepartout rode in the same carriage with his master, and a third passenger occupied a
5 seat opposite to them. This was Sir Francis Cromarty, now on his way to join his corps at Benares.

Sir Francis was a tall, fair man of fifty, who had greatly distinguished himself in the Sepoy revolt. He made India his home, only paying brief visits to England at rare intervals; and was almost as familiar
10 as a native[1] with the customs, history and character of India and its people. But Phileas Fogg, who was not travelling, but only describing a circumference, took no pains to inquire into these subjects; he was a solid body, traversing an orbit around the terrestrial globe, according to the laws of rational mechanics. He was at this moment calculating in
15 his mind the number of hours spent since his departure from London, and, had it been in his nature to make a useless demonstration, would have rubbed his hands for satisfaction.

Sir Francis Cromarty had observed the oddity of his travelling companion – although the only opportunity he had for studying him
20 had been while he was dealing the cards, and between two rubbers[2] – and questioned himself whether a human heart really beat beneath this cold exterior, and whether Phileas Fogg had any sense of the beauties of nature. The brigadier-general was free to mentally confess, that, of all the eccentric persons he had ever met, none was comparable to this
25 product of the exact sciences.

Phileas Fogg had not concealed from Sir Francis his design of going round the world, nor the circumstances under which he set out; and the general only saw in the wager a useless eccentricity and a lack of sound common sense. In the way this strange gentleman was going on,
30 he would leave the world without having done any good to himself or anybody else.

1 While we would not use this term in the twenty-first century, the narrator is saying that Sir Francis knows the country so well it is as if he had been born there.

2 They are playing a form of the card game called Bridge. A rubber is completed when one pair of players becomes first to win two games.

3 A narrow pass or gorge between mountains or hills.

An hour after leaving Bombay the train had passed the viaducts and the island of Salcette, and had got into the open country. At Callyan they reached the junction of the branch line which descends towards
35 south-eastern India by Kandallah and Pounah; and, passing Pauwell, they entered the defiles[3] of the mountains, with their basalt bases, and their summits crowned with thick and verdant forests. Phileas Fogg and Sir Francis Cromarty exchanged a few words from time to time, and now Sir Francis, reviving the conversation, observed, 'Some years
40 ago, Mr Fogg, you would have met with a delay at this point which would probably have lost you your wager.'

'How so, Sir Francis?'

'Because the railway stopped at the base of these mountains, which the passengers were obliged to cross in palanquins or on ponies to
45 Kandallah, on the other side.'

Jules Verne

Read more

If you're looking for journeys to even more adventurous places, Jules Verne's other novels in the *Voyages Extraordinaires* series – *Journey to the Centre of the Earth* and *Twenty Thousand Leagues Under the Sea* – are perfect for adventurous travellers!

Questions

1 The train was late. True or false? (1) **FP**
2 What is the name of the other passenger in their carriage? (1)
3 What is a synonym for 'concealed' (line 26)? (1)
4 What is meant by the phrase, 'the general only saw in the wager a useless eccentricity and a lack of sound common sense' (lines 28–29)? (2)
5 Which word is a synonym of 'verdant' (line 37)? (1)

   a   dry
   b   tall
   c   vast
   d   lush **FP**

Punctuation focus

Compound sentences

'Compound' means something made of two components. You might have heard the word in science lessons when conducting a chemistry experiment. Compound sentences are created in the same way and are built from two simple sentences. For example:

I like the colour blue + **my favourite colour is green**

=

I like the colour blue but my favourite colour is green.

All you need to make it a complete sentence is a conjunction and a punctuation mark to finish the sentence.

FANBOYS is a good **mnemonic** to help you remember the different conjunctions you can use:

For **A**nd **N**or **B**ut **O**r **Y**et **S**o

For more information on simple sentences, look back at page 12 in the Growing up chapter.

About the author

Ayesha Harruna Attah is a Ghanian-born writer living in Senegal. She has written two other successful books for adults but *The Deep Blue Between* (2020) is her first book for teenagers. Her books are often set against the backdrop of moments of historical importance in Africa.

Twin sisters Hassana and Husseina's home is in ruins after a brutal raid in the late-nineteenth century. Their escape route takes them to unfamiliar cities and cultures: Hassana to Accra in Ghana and Husseina to Bahia in Brazil. But even when they are apart, they are together through their shared dreams. In this extract, Husseina arrives in Brazil from West Africa with Yaya, a Candomblé priestess, who has saved her from slavery and baptised her Vitória.

The Deep Blue Between

Salvador de Bahia was like the yellow inside a flower. It was the moment after rainfall,
5 when the sun shone in full force. It was every skin shade in the world gathered in one place. As she
10 and Yaya rumbled along in a steam tram, she marvelled at how rich everything was around her. It was as if she was seeing, smelling and tasting for the first time. In Bahia, like a snake, Husseina moulted,
15 shedding the pain of her name and her past, and fully embracing Vitória.

When they had first arrived in Yaya's small orange brick box of a house resting on a hillside, a whole group was waiting for them. Mostly women, they had lined the house's corners with white and red blooms, had cooked beans, roasted a suckling pig, fried plantains, and doused
20 gari – which they called farina – with thick palm oil. They fussed over Vitória, clutching her to their chests and making sure her plate was never empty. She felt part of them, even though she didn't always understand what they said, especially when they spoke in rapid musical bursts. She loved that Yaya's neighbourhood was called Liberdade. It
25 made her feel as if she were kicking sand in the eyes of the people who had raided her village and kidnapped her. Now she lived in a place called Freedom. She was Vitória and she lived in Freedom.

1 A religion based on African beliefs, particularly popular in Brazil. It is a mixture of traditional Yoruba, Fon and Bantu beliefs which originated from different regions in Africa. Over time it has also incorporated some aspects of the Catholic faith.

Yaya had quickly climbed back into her old habits and wasted no time in planning and organising a Candomblé[1] ceremony, to be held at the
30 weekend. Vitória wondered when the novelty of the place would wear off. How different from Lagos Salvador was! Even Yaya was different here. It was clear the Lagos house was her dream house, inspired by some of the large homes Vitória had seen in Salvador. Here, Vitória wasn't sure Yaya could afford a house that big, but in Lagos, she could.
35 Here. Yaya bowed when she had visitors, her shoulders rounded in posture Vitória read as sadness. In Lagos, people bowed at Yaya's feet. Yaya shrank in Bahia, but there was something here that kept her coming back.

They arrived at the market. Vitória was used to markets being open
40 affairs but here the sellers had stalls under a big pavilion. Although they sold goods she was used to seeing – meat, fish, vegetables – some leaves and twigs looked different. Yaya went round stocking up on these unfamiliar items. When one woman offered Yaya kola nuts, Yaya shook her head, proudly proclaiming that she'd just come back from
45 the motherland with a fresh load. They went to the animal produce section, which reeked of raw flesh and chicken faeces. Yaya bought three white chickens, which the seller trussed at the feet and put in the basket Vitória was forced to carry. The only comfort she found was that their beaks had also been tied up. They bought so much food that they
50 had to hire two boys to carry their goods back to Yaya's house.

They'd arrived in Bahia just as the rains were starting, but it didn't look as if a dry season was ending. Back in Botu, everything would have been shrivelled and powdered in red dust. In Salvador, plants were still green and flowers blossomed in their pinks, yellows and oranges.
55 As Vitória climbed up the hill, she was surprised to find a colourful garden in front of a house not very different from Yaya's but inscribed on its wall were a moon and star. The etching was so faint, one could easily have missed it, but she hadn't. It had to be a mosque, which was surprising. It was like seeing a lion bathing in a pond. Out of place.
60 In Lagos, there were churches and mosques alike, but she hadn't seen anything like a mosque in Salvador. Churches stood on every corner. As were terrerios, temples tucked away in homes and in forests – as Yaya's was. She filed away the mosque in her mind and took up the basket of chickens, leaves and gnarled twigs.

Ayesha Harruna Attah

Questions

1 Find a quote that suggests Vitória and Yaya are made to feel welcome in Bahia. (1)
2 What neighbourhood do they live in and what does the word mean? (2)
3 What does 'trussed' (line 47) mean in the context of the extract? (1)
4 What is the house with the moon and the star on its wall? (1)

Punctuation tip: colons in lists

Here is an easy way of remembering what to include when you use a colon to start a list:

There are four things you need in order to use a colon to start a list: a number, some commas, an 'and' and confidence!

Research

Lagos, Nigeria and Salvador, Brazil are both cities that are mentioned in the extract above. Get to know one or both of these cities a little better by researching the following:

- Find it on a map – what do you notice about its location? For example, is it on the coast or inland?
- What languages are spoken there?
- What is it famous for? For example, a trade or a food.
- Has anything historically important happened there?
- What does it look like now and how did it look in the nineteenth century?

Talking point

In small groups, discuss the route you would take to go around the world in 80 days. You should cover the following:

- which specific countries or cities you'd visit (you should have at least one in every continent)
- any sights or wonders of the world you'd like to see
- how you would travel
- what you would need to take with you.

Writing questions on *Around the World in 80 Days*

1   In your own words, explain why Sir Francis knows India so well. (2)
2   What do you think Phileas Fogg does that makes Sir Francis notice 'the oddity of his travelling companion'? Refer to the text in your answer. (3)
3   Read lines 32–45. How does the author make it clear that the train is now in a rural setting? (4)

Writing questions on *The Deep Blue Between*

1   Read lines 1–9. How has the author created an effective description of Salvador? (6)
2   In your own words, list three things that are different in Salvador compared to Lagos. (3)
3   How does the author make the description of the mosque seem significant to the reader? (4)

Speaking and listening focus
Character development

In groups, choose one person to be the 'character' to enter conscience alley. The character is at a crossroads in their life, either a literal one on a journey (choosing which way to go) or an emotional one (they're not sure what option to choose). Decide what type of crossroads it is or use a character who faces a complex choice from a book you've read.

Stand in two parallel lines to create a conscience alley. The character walks down the alley and, as they do, everyone in the line will share their advice about which is the right way to go and why. At the end of the alley the character must make their choice and explain why they made their decision and whose advice they took.

Thematic focus

Phileas Fogg is a gentleman, travelling on a train with a valet (a servant). Husseina is a young girl walking back from the market carrying three chickens for a priestess. Compare the status of our two main characters by finding quotes in the text which suggest their position and then sum up their status with just one **adjective** in the table below:

Phileas Fogg	Husseina
'Passepartout rode in the same carriage with his master'	'put in the basket Vitória was forced to carry'
Adjective to describe status:	Adjective to describe status:

Extended writing questions

You will now be writing an extended answer about an extract. Write your answer in three PEEA paragraphs, using evidence from the text to support your ideas. (See page 179 in the Exam skills for an explanation of PEEA.)

Here are some tips for writing extended answers:

- Read the questions carefully.
- Use the three foci in your topic sentences for the three paragraphs.
- It might help you to find your evidence for each before you start writing.
- Use connectives like 'and', 'furthermore', 'however' and 'additionally' to expand your explanations.

1 Phileas Fogg is a gentleman. How can you tell from Extract 1?

   Consider the use of vocabulary, the character's actions and other characters' reactions to him.

OR

2 How does the author create a sense of newness in Extract 2?

   Refer to vocabulary, imagery and sentence construction.

OR

3 Write a letter as Sir Francis telling a friend about his encounter with Phileas Fogg on the train. You should explore:
   - Sir Francis' first impressions of Phileas Fogg
   - his thoughts and feelings about the wager
   - what happened after the extract finished.

About the author

David Morton is an Australian playwright, designer and director. He is the Creative Director of the Dead Puppet Society, which builds stage productions and events around incredible puppetry to create true visual theatre.

The Wider Earth (2018) started as a reimagining of Charles Darwin's voyage on the *HMS Beagle* to discover new creatures and lands, using puppetry. What Darwin discovered on this voyage changed the course of scientific thinking, advanced ideas about evolution and thus created a conflict between scientific and religious belief. Here Darwin discusses his thoughts with the ship's captain, Fitzroy.

The Wider Earth

The inside of the Beagle's hull is littered with specimens. FITZROY watches Charles work.

FITZROY   You're turning my ship into quite an ark.

CHARLES They're all the most curious creatures, Robert.

5 FITZROY   Perfectly created for curious islands.

CHARLES There's no doubt it's new land. Not long ago there would have been nothing but ocean here.

FITZROY   They were recently populated then?

CHARLES Must have been. But the creatures all bear remarkable
10   similarities to those of the continent. I think they might have been castaways.

FITZROY   You're saying a two-hundred-pound-tortoise somehow made its way across five hundred miles of open ocean?

CHARLES There are so many riddles I can't explain. This iguana
15   feeds at sea. Its cousin in the Amazon lives entirely on land. Perhaps it learnt to swim. But that can't explain the shrunken wings of the cormorants. Why would God create such creatures?

FITZROY   Man desires dogs and pigeons in all number of fancy
20   varieties, why should the Lord not be afforded the same want?

CHARLES There's more. The locals knew which island these tortoises came from just by the shape of their shells. It's the same with the species of mockingbird. Only slight differences
25   from one another, but marked.

FITZROY   I'm sure you'll find sense in it.

CHARLES Why would God put such creative energy into minutely changing the appearance of animals on such tiny islands?

30 FITZROY Because He populates His creation as He sees fit, and that is the way of it.

CHARLES I know that.

FITZROY Then acknowledge it.

CHARLES I can't. Not yet.

FITZROY Why not?

35 CHARLES If you send a trained naturalist into the field, every new discovery will reassure him of what he already thinks he knows. Send a young man who knows nothing and there's no telling what he might find.

FITZROY Who said that?

40 CHARLES Someone much wiser than me.

FITZROY Curiosity for its sake is not wisdom, Charles.

CHARLES I need to work.

FITZROY leaves CHARLES alone in his cabin.

CHARLES sits with the creatures late into the night as the Beagle charts a
45 *course into the Pacific Ocean.*

He turns the fossil from the Andes over and over in his hands.

He holds food above the tortoises.

The saddleback tortoise can reach, the dome tortoise cannot.

CHARLES collects his journal and goes to sit in the bow.

As he thinks, the point of light appears and dances in the night sky.

A dome tortoise wanders the cosmos.

Its shell becomes a horizon.

50 *Earthquakes raise the ground.*

The new peak is the raised shell of a saddleback tortoise.

A cormorant soars through the air above it.

Its wing becomes a peninsula.

The ocean wears the wing down.

55 *The shrunken wing belongs to a cormorant that soars beneath the waves.*

Volcanoes push land out of the ocean.

They become the raised scales of an iguana.

The eye of the iguana becomes the Earth.

The Earth becomes the point of light.

60 *The point of light begins to draw the tree of life.*

Before it fully forms, the tree is lost in the chaos of its own blinding light.

CHARLES slams his journal closed and climbs back to the deck.

David Morton

Questions

1 What adjective does Charles use to describe the creatures and Fitzroy use to describe the islands? (1)
2 How heavy is the tortoise Fitzroy mentions? (1)
3 What is the definition of 'minutely' (line 27)? (1)
4 In the final part of the scene, what do the volcanoes become? (1)

Text features

Narrative structures

The Hero's Journey is a story structure which dates from the tales of ancient mythology. Charles Darwin, even though he is based on a real-life person, goes through steps of *The Hero's Journey* during the play. Firstly, the hero is called to an adventure. They may be given supernatural aid or be helped by a guardian before they cross the threshold into the unknown. Here is where the adventure really starts. After tackling challenges and temptations, transformation and a near-fatal abyss, the hero eventually makes it back to the known world. Upon their return, they are gifted with knowledge or a new status.

Stories that follow the same structure include *Theseus and the Minotaur*, and *The Quest for the Holy Grail* in the tales of King Arthur. Try to think of three more stories with this quest formula.

Language focus

Stage directions

It's important to remember that scripts are written to be performed. In this case, Morton was aiming to create visual theatre, so it makes it even more important that when reading this drama script, we imagine it on stage.

Stage directions, written by the writer to guide the director and actors, help readers too. They make it clear what the lighting is like or the sound effects or even how a scene changes from one place to another. For example, this scene shows a change of set and lighting:

CHARLES sits with the creatures late into the night as the Beagle charts a course into the Pacific Ocean.

The writer has kept in these ideas, even if a director or actor does not use them in the final production, to help their script come to life, so pay attention to the clues they offer to the reader.

For more information about stage directions which feature lighting notes, look back at page 52 in the Technology and communication chapter.

Writing questions on *The Wider Earth*

1 Why does Fitzroy compare his ship to an ark? (2)
2 What is the significance of the 'point of light' (line 47)? Refer closely to the text in your answer. (4)
3 What are your impressions of Charles Darwin from these two scenes? (4)
4 The playwright wanted to create visual theatre in this play. In what ways did he achieve it? (2)

Extended writing questions

You will now be writing an extended answer to the question below. Write your answer in three PEEA paragraphs, using evidence from the text to support your ideas. (See page 179 in the Exam skills for an explanation of the PEEA technique.)

Here are some tips for writing extended answers:

● Read the questions carefully.
● Use the three foci in your topic sentences for the three paragraphs.
● It might help you to find your evidence for each before you start writing.

● Use connectives 'and', 'furthermore', 'however' and 'additionally' to expand your explanations.

How does the playwright, David Morton, make this scene engaging and thought-provoking?

Consider these three points:

● the presentation of Charles in the first and second parts of the scene
● dramatic effects, including through the use of lighting to create visual theatre
● what the scene suggests about the role of Fitzroy in relation to Charles.

Context

Orwell was living and writing through a period of great change. The devastating impact of the First World War decimated national economies and a generation of young men. While Orwell believed that everything that was made and earned should be shared with an entire community, extreme political regimes of the 1930s thought the opposite. Both war and this conflict of ideas inspired Orwell's fiction and non-fiction writing.

In the late 1920s, he began exploring the poorest parts of London and Paris, rejecting his privileged background so that he could immerse himself in a new way of living and record his impressions in a memoir, *Down and Out in Paris and London* (1933).

Down and Out in Paris and London

1   A simple wooden shoe, similar to a clog.

The Rue Du Coq d'Or, Paris, seven in the morning. A succession of furious, choking yells from the street. Madame Monce, who kept the little hotel opposite mine, had come out onto the pavement to address a lodger on the third floor. Her bare feet were stuck into sabots[1] and
5   her grey hair was streaming down…

Thereupon a whole variegated chorus of yells, as windows were flung open on every side and half the street joined in the quarrel. They shut up abruptly ten minutes later, when a squadron of cavalry rode past and people stopped shouting to look at them.

10   I sketch this scene, just to convey something of the spirit of the Rue du Coq d'Or. Not that quarrels were the only thing that happened there – but still, we seldom got through the morning without at least one outburst of this description. Quarrels, and the desolate cries of street hawkers, and the shouts of children chasing orange-peel over the
15   cobbles, and at night loud singing and the sour reek of the refuse-carts, made up the atmosphere of the street.

It was a very narrow street – a ravine of tall leprous houses, lurching towards one another in queer attitudes, as though they had all been frozen in the act of collapse. All the houses were hotels and packed to
20   the tiles with lodgers… At the foot of the hotels were tiny bistros, where you could be drunk for the equivalent of a shilling. On Saturday nights about a third of the male population of the quarter was drunk… At night the policemen would only come through the street two together. It was a fairly rackety place. And yet amid the noise and dirt lived the
25   usual respectable French shopkeepers, bakers and laundresses and the like, keeping themselves to themselves and quietly piling up the small fortunes. It was quite a representative Paris slum.

> **2** So ingrained it cannot be changed.

My hotel was called the Hôtel des Trois Moineaux. It was a dark, rickety warren of five storeys, cut up by wooden partitions into forty
30 rooms. The rooms were small and inveterately[2] dirty, for there was no maid, and Madame F., the patronne, had no time to do any sweeping. The walls were as thin as matchwood, and to hide the cracks they had been covered with layer after layer of pink paper, which had come loose and housed innumerable bugs.

> **3** A great public sacrifice (in Ancient Greece or Rome).

35 Near the ceiling long lines of bugs marched all day like columns of soldiers, and at night came down ravenously hungry, so that one had to get up every few hours
40 and kill them in hecatombs[3]. Sometimes when the bugs got too bad one used to burn sulphur and drive them into the next room; whereupon the lodger next door
45 would retort by having his room sulphured, and drive the bugs back. It was a dirty place, but homelike, for Madame F. and her husband were good sorts. The rent
50 of the rooms varied between thirty and fifty francs a week…

There were eccentric characters in the hotel. The Paris slums are a gathering-place for eccentric people – people who have fallen into solitary, half-mad grooves of life and given
55 up trying to be normal or decent. Poverty frees them from ordinary standards of behaviour, just as money frees people from work. Some of the lodgers in our hotel lived lives that were curious beyond words.

George Orwell

Questions

1 What is the definition of 'variegated' (line 6)? (1)
2 Identify the language techniques used in 'a ravine of tall leprous houses' (line 17) and explain their effect. (4)
3 In your own words, explain what is meant by 'It was a fairly rackety place' (line 24)? (2)
4 How many rooms were in the Hôtel des Trois Moineaux? (1)
5 Read lines 28–51. How has the author created such a vivid description of the Hôtel des Trois Moineaux (meaning 'three sparrows')? Refer closely to the text in your answer. (4)

Text features

Small details make a big difference when describing a setting. Orwell describes one of the smallest: bugs! By using small details, he is able to bring the Rue du Coq d'Or to life.

Orwell also does this by including the sights, sounds and smells of the place. By using sensory description, we feel like we are in his shoes.

He also describes the place at different times of the day, showing how its atmosphere shifts and changes.

By the end of the extract, we know the street inside out because he has zoomed in and out from all different angles, using his pen like a camera.

Language focus

Narrative hooks

George Orwell opens his memoir with this extract. It hooks the reader in with simple information: the place and time. As a reader, we know exactly when and where he is but also want to know why it is of such importance, which makes us want to read on. But **narrative hooks** come in all shapes and sizes. See if you can spot a variation of these on the first page of the book you are currently reading:

- Direct speech, for example: *Get a move on!*
- Atmospheric description, for example: *Like a glowing eye, the moon stared down...*
- Ambiguity, for example: *He started with the North Star.*
- Short sentence, for example: *It was over in a moment.*
- Direct address, for example: *Have you ever tried being your sister for a day?*

Drama focus

How do you travel around the world on a ship with hundreds of creatures in a theatre? That is the conundrum a set designer must solve and now it's your turn! Design the set for the drama extract in this chapter. You may have access to a digital design programme to create your set or you may prefer to make a 3-D model (old shoe boxes can be useful for this).

Writing task

You are going to write a description that captures the atmosphere of somewhere you enjoyed visiting. Here are some tips:

- Use small details to imply. For example, instead of telling a reader there is a dusty road, show the reader through sensory description or **figurative** language.
- Just like Orwell, zoom in and out on tiny details and general descriptions of the area.
- Describe the place at different times of day. This will give you a chance to describe the changing atmosphere.

Opportunities to zoom in and out, as well as describe the place at different times of the day (just like Orwell), are in the plan below:

Paragraph 1

Introduce the place in the morning.

Paragraph 2

Describe the area.

Paragraph 3

Zoom in on a small detail.

Paragraph 4

End your piece by describing what it's like at night.

Time to write

Write a description that captures the atmosphere of somewhere you enjoyed visiting.

Putting pen to paper

Now try one of the writing tasks below:

1   Describe a place that is special to you.
2   Write a description about a walk through a city.
3   Write a description of a historical place.

Spelling tip: suffixes

To add the **suffix** 'ous' correctly to words ending in 'our', you must drop the 'u':

odour + ous = odorous

glamour + ous = glamorous

humour + ous = humorous

Peer review (editing/drafting)
Reviewing your writing

Swap your writing with a partner. Read each other's work carefully, looking at:

- your favourite moments of description – what makes those examples so effective?
- the way ideas/points of view are expressed – are they clear?
- how the description is structured – do the ideas link well?

Find two positive things that would improve the writing in your view. Share these with your partner.

Edit your work, considering these changes and correcting any spelling or punctuation errors.

Wider reading

If you want to read more about terrific travels and journeys, have a look at these brilliant books and awesome authors:

- *The Odyssey* by Geraldine McCraughrean
- *A Walk in the Woods* by Bill Bryson*
- *A Wrinkle in Time* by Madeline L'Engle
- *A Jigsaw of Fire and Stars* by Yaba Badoe
- *The ABC Murders* or *Murder on the Orient Express* by Agatha Christie*
- *Sophie Someone* by Hayley Long
- *The Adventures of Tintin* by Hergé

*Choose these titles for a more challenging read!

Book review

Prepare a news report about an event that takes place on a journey from a book you have read recently. It might be one from the wider reading list above.

Ask a partner to listen to your news report. What does your partner think of the event? Does it make them want to read the book?

5 Love and heartbreak

Aims

- **Reading focus**: Inference
- **Writing focus**: Giving advice and recommendations in a letter
- **Speaking and listening focus**: Varying tone and expression
- **Language focus**: Imagery, sonnet structure and rhetorical questions
- **Drama focus**: Improvisation

Context

Butterflies in the stomach, birds tweeting and hearts skipping a beat. Love. Is it really all it's cracked up to be? Well, writers definitely think so. For thousands of years, authors, playwrights and poets have been inspired by every form of love and, of course, heartbreak.

In this chapter, you will be thinking with your head and heart, uncovering the hidden feelings of some beloved characters by analysing single words and imagery. You will also explore how small details, like an innocent question mark, can make a big difference, especially when it comes to romance. But it's not all mushy stuff; we will be looking at the science behind crushes too and asking if it's all a figment of our imagination. Finally, you will give some advice to a poet who is on the brink of a break-up.

Malorie Blackman OBE is a British writer who was Children's Laureate from 2013–2015. She writes for television as well as being a novelist, and focuses on social and ethical issues that affect young people. She wrote the dystopian novel *Noughts and Crosses* (2001) to explore racism and the legacy of slavery.

In this extract, Callum, a Nought, has started at a new school that is for the higher-status Crosses. His friend Sephy, a Cross, joined him at lunch but he turned his back on her.

Noughts and Crosses

'I DON'T UNDERSTAND…' The words erupted from me in an angry rush, heading for the sky and beyond.

I sat there for I don't know how long, furious thoughts darting around my head like bluebottles, my head aching, my chest hurting. Until I suddenly
5   snapped out of it with a jolt. Someone was watching me. I turned sharply and a shock like static electricity zapped through my body.

Sephy was further down the beach, standing perfectly still as the wind whipped around her, making her jacket and skirt billow out. We were about seven metres apart – or seven million light years, depending on how
10 you looked at it. Then Sephy turned around and started to walk away.

'Sephy, wait.' I jumped to my feet and sprinted after her.

She carried on walking.

'Sephy, please. Wait.' I caught up with her and pulled around to face me. She pulled away from my grasp like I was contaminated.

15 'Yes?'

'Don't be like that?' I pleaded.

'Like what?'

I glared at her. 'Aren't you going to stay?'

'I don't think so.'

20 'Why not?'

At first I thought she wasn't going to answer.

'I don't want to stay where I'm not wanted.' Sephy turned around again. I ran to stand in front of her.

'I did it for your own good.'

25 A strange expression flitted across her face. 'Did you? Was it my good or your own you were thinking about?'

'Maybe a bit of both,' I admitted.

'Maybe a lot of one and none of the other,' Sephy contradicted.

'I'm sorry – ok?'

30 'So am I. I'll see you, Callum.' Sephy tried to walk around me again, but I moved directly into her path. Fear tore at my insides. If she left now, that would be the end. Funny how a few hours ago, that'd been exactly what I was wishing for.

'Sephy, wait!'

35 'For what?'

'H-how about if you and I go up to Celebration Wood this Saturday?' We could have a picnic.'

Sephy's eyes lit up although she tried her best to hide it. I breathed an inward sigh of relief although I was careful not to show it.

40 'Celebration Wood…?'

'Yeah. Just you and me.'

'Are you sure you won't be ashamed to be seen with me?' Sephy asked.

'Don't be ridiculous.'

Sephy regarded me. 'What time shall I meet you?' she said at last.

45 'How about ten-thirty at the train station? I'll meet you on the platform.'

'Ok.' Sephy turned away.

'Where're you going now?' I asked.

'Home.'

50 'Why don't you stay a while?'

'I don't want to disturb you.'

'Sephy, get off it,' I snapped.

'Get off what?' You're a snob, Callum. And I never realised it until today,' Sephy snapped, just as angry. 'I thought you were better than that, above 55 all that nonsense. But you're like everyone else. "Crosses and noughts shouldn't be seen together. Crosses and noughts shouldn't be friends. Crosses and noughts shouldn't even live on the same planet together."'

'That's rubbish!' I fumed. 'I don't believe any of that, you know I don't.'

'Do I?' Sephy tilted her head to one side as she continued to scrutinize 60 me. 'Well, if you're not a snob, you're a hypocrite, which is even worse. I'm ok to talk to as long as no one sees us, as long as no one knows.'

'Don't talk to me like that…'

'Why? Does the truth hurt?' asked Sephy. 'Which one is it, Callum? Are you a snob or a hypocrite?'

65 'Get lost, Sephy.'

'With pleasure.'

And this time, when Sephy walked away I didn't try to stop her. I just watched her leave.

Malorie Blackman

Questions

1 Where does the extract take place? (1)
2 What language technique is used in the phrase 'thoughts darting around my head like bluebottles' (lines 3–4)? (1)
3 Where does Callum suggest they go on Saturday? (1)
4 What does 'scrutinize' (line 59) mean? (1)
   a to screw up eyes
   b to look at closely
   c to talk intensely
   d to disbelieve **FP**
5 What does Sephy say is 'even worse' than being a snob? (1)

Grammar focus
Using verbs for descriptive dialogue

Searching for hidden or **implied** meanings can feel like looking for a needle in a haystack, but there is a strategy! **Verbs** describing how a character speaks can be clues to these meanings.

On first reading, verbs like 'erupted' might make you think Callum is angry but there are clues to more loving feelings too, such as 'pleaded'.

You can analyse these clue-like verbs in your comprehension answers. It can add relevant detail to your explanation.

In composition, verbs offer an easy way both to add **description** to **dialogue** and show off your **vocabulary** range.

Write another ten lines of dialogue between Callum and Sephy using the following verbs to show the reader how they're feeling:

> *hollered   demurred   effused   quipped   gushed   hissed   accused*

About the author

Charlotte Brontë (1816–1855) was an English novelist and poet, and she also worked as a governess, just like her heroine. Along with her sisters, Emily and Mary, she initially published her novels under a gender-ambiguous **pseudonym** because the perception of female authors was poor at the time. Soon the sisters admitted the books were theirs and became much celebrated.

In Charlotte Brontë's *Jane Eyre* (1847), Jane is employed as a governess at mysterious Mr Rochester's house. They have fallen in love and are about to get married when a deep, dark secret is revealed: he already has a wife and she's locked in a secret room in the house. In this extract, the two characters argue.

1 Mr Rochester describes his wife, Bertha Mason, as a maniac but is she really? Many critics believe Mr Rochester may be to blame for her supposed 'madness'. Even though he claims that mental illness runs in her family, he has betrayed her and kept her isolated for years.

Jane Eyre

'Jane, you understand what I want of you? Just this promise – "I will be yours, Mr Rochester."'

'Mr Rochester, I will *not* be yours.'

Another long silence.

5 'Jane!' recommenced he, with a gentleness that broke me down with grief, and turned me stone-cold with ominous terror – for this still voice was the pant of a lion rising – 'Jane, do you mean to go one way in the world, and to let me go another?'

'I do.'

10 'Jane' (bending towards and embracing me,) 'do you mean it now?'

'I do.'

'And now?' softly kissing my forehead and cheek.

'I do' – extricating myself from restraint rapidly and completely.

'Oh Jane, this is bitter! This – this is wicked. It would not be wicked to
15 love me.'

'It would be to obey you.'

A wild look raised his brows – crossed his features: he rose; but he forbore yet. I laid my hand on the back of the chair for support: I shook, I feared – but I resolved.

20 'One instant, Jane. Give me one glance to my horrible life when you are gone. All happiness will be torn away with you. What then is left? For a wife I have but the maniac[1] upstairs: as well might you refer me to some corpse in yonder churchyard. What shall I do, Jane? Where turn I
25 for a companion or some hope?'

'Do as I do: trust in God and yourself. Believe in heaven. Hope to meet again there.'

'Then you do not yield?'

'No.' [...]

30 His fury was wrought to the highest: he must yield to it for a moment, whatever followed; he crossed the floor and seized my arm and grasped my waist. He seemed to devour me with his flaming glance. My eye rose to his; and while I looked in his fierce face I gave an involuntary sigh; his grip was painful, and my overtaxed strength almost
35 exhausted…

'It is you, spirit – with will and energy, and virtue and purity – that I want. Oh! Jane!'

As he said this, he released me from his clutch, and only looked at me. The look was far worse to resist than the frantic strain: only an idiot,
40 however, would have succumbed now. I had dared and baffled his fury; I must elude his sorrow. I retired to the door.

'You are going, Jane?'

'I am going, sir.'

'You are leaving me?'

45 'Yes.'

'You will not come. You will not be my comforter, my rescuer? My deep love, my wild woe, my frantic prayer, are all nothing to you?'

What unutterable pathos² was in his voice! How hard it was to reiterate firmly, 'I am going.'

50 'Jane!'

'Mr Rochester!'

'Withdraw, then – I consent – but remember, you leave me here in anguish. Go up to your own room; think over all I have said, and, Jane, cast a glance on my sufferings – think of me.'

55 He turned away; he threw himself on the sofa. 'Oh Jane! My hope – my love – my life!' broke in anguish from his lips. Then came a deep, strong sob.

I had already gained the door; but, reader, I walked back – walked back as determinedly as I had retreated. I knelt down by him; I turned his face from the cushion to me; I kissed his cheek; I smoothed his hair
60 with my hand.

'God bless you, my dear master!' I said.

Charlotte Brontë

---

2 A quality that evokes pity or sadness.

Questions

1 Read lines 5–6. Choose the pair of adjectives that best describe how is Jane feeling. (1)
  a happy / celebratory
  b upset / relieved
  c sad / scared
  d angry / uneasy (FP)

2 Read lines 17–19. What is the effect of the punctuation in these lines? (1)

3 What is the definition of 'consent' (line 52)? (1)

4 What person is the text written in? (1)

5 Read lines 62–63, paying close attention to the punctuation. Write a word or phrase that describes how Mr Rochester is speaking. (1)

Punctuation tip: lists with semicolons

Commas divide a list of single items:

I have read Jane Eyre, Wuthering Heights *and* Agnes Grey.

Semicolons divide a list of phrases:

I knelt down by him; I turned his face from the cushion to me; I kissed his cheek; I smoothed his hair with my hand.

Research

Jane Eyre and the Brontë sisters' work are what you might call 'classics'. Use the questions below to understand why their work continues to be read centuries later.

● What were the names of Charlotte's sisters and what books did they write?
● What were the pseudonyms that the Brontë sisters used and why did they use them?
● How did Charlotte Brontë's life mirror that of her heroine, Jane?

Talking point

Both extracts are written in **first person**, so we only hear one side... until now! Work in pairs. One person will be on Callum or Jane's side, the other person will take Sephy or Mr Rochester's side. Discuss the following questions based on the side you are on. Give each other 30 seconds to explain and give evidence for your answers. Listen carefully to each other's point of view and then respond.

● What did the characters want from this conversation?
● Who won this argument?
● Who lost this argument?
● What does the future hold for their relationship?

Do you have opposing views or are they surprisingly similar? Did you discover anything you hadn't thought of before this?

Writing questions on *Noughts and Crosses*

1 Why do you think Callum has come to the beach? (2)
2 In your own words, explain the meaning of 'a shock like static electricity zapped through my body' (line 6) in the context of what is happening at this point in the text. (2)
3 a Find two quotations that show Sephy feels more for Callum than her words suggest. (2)
   b Explain what these quotations suggest about Sephy's feelings. (4)
4 Looking at the passage as whole, what impressions do you have of Callum and Sephy? Support your ideas with details from the text. (4)

Writing questions on *Jane Eyre*

1   How do Jane's feelings and emotions change throughout the extract? Explain your ideas with reference to details from the passage. (4)
2   What is your impression of Mr Rochester? (4)
3   Looking at the passage as a whole, what is your impression of Mr Rochester and Jane's relationship? (2)
4   Look at the punctuation in this extract. Find two examples where you think it is used successfully and explain its effect. (4)
5   Explain why you think Jane walked back, using specific evidence from the text. (3)

Speaking and listening focus
Tone and expression

Small details can make a big difference. Punctuation can reveal so much about a writer's **purpose** and a character's motivations if we consider the function of the punctuation mark. For instance, a comma creates a short pause but a full stop creates a much longer one. It really helps to read a text aloud so you can spot these clues. In small groups, read these examples aloud one by one and discuss what emotions you think they create:

Different punctuation marks create a different **tone** in writing and **expression** in speaking so the meaning can be totally changed. You could get into a lot of trouble in love without the right punctuation marks!

Look back at the two extracts. Can you alter any of the punctuation to change the meaning?

79

Thematic focus

Some things never change! Even though the extracts were written over 150 years apart, both extracts feature arguments, but underneath it all we can tell the characters clearly have romantic feelings for each other. Nevertheless, the authors use language and structure in different ways to present these arguments. A Venn diagram is a useful way to organise your ideas when comparing the texts.

Copy and complete the Venn diagram below by adding your own thoughts and ideas about the extracts.

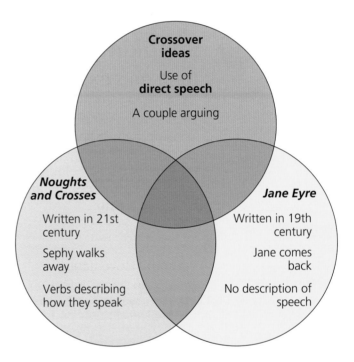

(See page 179 in the Exam skills chapter for an explanation of PEEA.)

Extended writing questions

You will now be writing an extended answer about an extract. Write your answer in three PEEA paragraphs, using evidence from the text to support your ideas. (See page 179 in the Exam skills chapter for an explanation of PEEA.)

Here are some tips for writing extended answers:

- Read the questions carefully.
- Use the three foci in your topic sentences for the three paragraphs.
- It might help you to find your evidence for each before you start writing.
- Use connectives like 'and', 'furthermore', 'however' and 'additionally' to expand your explanations.

1 How does the author show the characters' confusion in Extract 1 from *Noughts and Crosses*?

You should focus on vocabulary, punctuation and imagery.

OR

2 How does the author show power and control in Extract 2 from *Jane Eyre*?

You should focus on vocabulary, punctuation and imagery.

OR

3 Retell the *Noughts and Crosses* extract from Sephy's point of view.

You should consider what she feels when she sees Callum, her thoughts about what he says and why she walks away.

Language focus
Inference through imagery

Deeper meanings can be hidden by writers in imagery too. **Imagery** means the combination of words a writer uses to create a picture in the reader's mind. Figurative techniques can do this, but it can also be created through vocabulary choice. Imagery is useful for writers trying to explain often indescribable feelings, so by comparing one thing to another it can help readers understand what the writer means. By considering imagery, you can unlock the meaning of a piece of writing. Here are some examples of imagery with their possible meanings:

Imagery	Meaning
Her words burnt and scorched the air, as she turned away in a blaze of red hair.	The imagery of fire suggests that she is angry with the speaker because the language used implies damage and danger.
My grandparents' mottled hands intertwined across the table, their veins tracing a pattern like bark on a mighty oak.	Comparing their skin to a tree's bark implies that they have grown together and their relationship is long-lasting, just like the 'mighty oak'.

Tips for improving

Antonyms can be just as handy as **synonyms**. Shakespeare's famous play *Romeo* and *Juliet* is full of **oxymorons**, such as 'cold fire' and 'sweet sorrow'. Instead of using a word that means the same as one you want to change, try the opposite for more interesting descriptions.

Context

You will have noticed that the portrayal of the female characters in the two extracts are very different. This is when it is important to acknowledge the context in which the text was written. When Brontë was writing in the nineteenth century, women's rights were barely recognised and their husbands controlled any money or property they brought to the marriage. Even though Jane has earnt her own money as a governess, her status is much lower than that of Mr Rochester as his fiancée. The control Mr Rochester exerts over Bertha Mason could be considered a metaphor for the lower status of women at this time when compared to men.

About the author

William Shakespeare (1564–1616) was an English playwright, poet and actor. His plays and sonnets have endured for centuries thanks to their memorable characters, plots and lines, and they have been adapted into hundreds of films, stage and television productions. You will often hear him called 'the Bard' which meant 'poet' at the time he was writing.

Consider how religious imagery is used to show the strength of first love in the extract from *Romeo and Juliet* (1595).

The Capulet family and the Montague family are great rivals. Romeo Montague has gatecrashed a Capulet party with his friends. He spots Juliet Capulet across the room. Not knowing who she is, he makes his way towards her.

1 A religious monument, a place to worship a deity or saint.

2 Pilgrims travel long distances to visit places of religious significance.

3 Saints are people who are recognised as having a closeness to God or great holiness. Pilgrims show devotion to them by praying.

Romeo and Juliet

ROMEO [taking Juliet's hand]

If I profane with my unworthiest hand

This holy shrine[1], the gentle sin is this:

My lips, two blushing pilgrims[2], ready stand

To smooth that rough touch with a tender kiss.

JULIET

Good pilgrim, you do wrong your hand too much,

Which mannerly devotion shows in this,

For saints[3] have hands that pilgrims' hands do touch,

And palm to palm is holy palmers' kiss.

ROMEO

Have not saints lips, and holy palmers too?

JULIET

Ay, pilgrim, lips that they must use in prayer.

ROMEO

O, then dear saint, let lips do what hands do;

They pray: Grant thou, lest faith turn to despair.

JULIET

Saints do not move, though grant for prayers' sake.

ROMEO

Then move not while my prayer's effect I take. [kisses her]

William Shakespeare

Research

William Shakespeare is probably the most famous playwright in the world. Use the following questions to guide your research on his life and work.

- Where was Shakespeare born and what is it like now?
- Who performed his plays and where were they performed when they were first written?
- How would watching a play be different in Shakespearean times compared to now?
- Shakespeare is believed to have written around 36 plays, but did Shakespeare write all the plays he's credited with?

1 As well as referring to a bar in the Wild West, this phrase can also mean a final opportunity to be successful after a number of failures.

'Quickdraw'

I wear the two, the mobile and the landline phones,

like guns, slung from the pockets on my hips. I'm all

alone. You ring, quickdraw, your voice a pellet

in my ear, and hear me groan.

5 You've wounded me.

Next time, you speak after the tone. I twirl the phone,

Then squeeze the trigger of my tongue, wide of the mark.

You choose your spot, then blast me

through the heart.

10 And this love, high noon, calamity, hard liquor

in the old Last Chance saloon¹. I show the mobile

to the sheriff; in my boot, another one's

concealed. You text them both at once. I reel.

Down on my knees, I fumble for the phone,

15 read the silver bullets of your kiss. Take this…

and this…and this….and this…and this…

Carol Ann Duffy

Questions

1 What does the speaker compare the two phones to? (1)
2 Find a quote that suggests the phone conversation is an argument. (1)
3 What else is 'concealed' in the boot? (1)
4 What language technique is used in the phrase 'the silver bullets of your kiss' (line 15)? (1)

Read more

Read Elizabeth Barrett Browning's 'How Do I Love Thee? Sonnet 43' – it's a Petrarchan sonnet. Can you spot the structural differences to Shakespeare's sonnet?

Text features
Sonnet structure

Did you notice anything about the structure of the *Romeo and Juliet* extract? It's a hidden **sonnet**! Well-known for his love sonnets, as well as plays, Shakespeare hid this sonnet here to show how much they loved each other from first sight.

Sonnets are almost always about love, but they come in many forms, such as Petrarchan and Spenserian, as well as Shakespearean. Some modern poets, like Simon Armitage, have played with the form too. A Shakespearean sonnet follows this structure:

- 14 lines long, made up of three quatrains (three four-line sections) and a rhyming couplet (two rhyming lines)
- a **rhyme scheme** of ABABCDCDEFEFGG
- written in **iambic pentameter** (lines of 10 syllables with alternating stresses)
- a **volta** (a turn or change) which occurs at any point.

Language focus
Wild West imagery

Duffy's inspiration for the imagery in her poem is the Wild West. The American frontier was made infamous in classic Hollywood Western movies featuring gun-toting cowboys, which exaggerated the romance and anarchy for entertainment while ignoring the historical facts. Ordinary objects and situations are heightened in emotion and drama in the poem by using this theme.

By using the same type of imagery throughout, Duffy has created an extended metaphor. For more on extended metaphors look at page 133 in the Different people, different perspectives chapter.

Enjambment is a structural device that poets often use. You can identify this device by the lack of punctuation at the end of a line or stanza in a poem. For example:

You choose your spot, then blast me
through the heart.

Can you find any other examples of enjambment in the poem?

The effect of enjambment really depends on the meaning of the poem it's included in, but usually it's to build pace or emphasise the word at the end of the line or the beginning of the next. Why do you think Duffy used it for the lines above, and any others you have found?

Writing questions on 'Quickdraw'

1 a Find two quotations from the poem which describe communication. (2)

 b How does the speaker feel in each quotation? (4)

2 Explain your understanding of 'and this…and this…and this…and this…' (line 16) in the context of what is happening at this point of the poem. (2)

3 What is your main impression of the speaker? Explain your ideas with reference to details in the poem. (4)

4 In what ways is the use of Wild West imagery successful? (3)

About the author

Hannah Devlin has a PhD biomedical imaging from the University of Oxford. She is the Science Correspondent for the *Guardian* and hosts a weekly podcast about science.

It's not just artists who are obsessed with love – scientists are too. Whether it's chemicals bubbling or neurons sparking, they're still trying to work out how and why we fall in love.

1 An expert in the study of the human race and its culture, society and biology.

'What is love – and is it all in the mind?'

We look at the science behind romance, from the brain chemicals that make us swoon to how to know when you've met 'the one'.

What do you get when you fall in love?

5 We crave romantic love like nothing else, we'll make unimaginable sacrifices for it and it can take us from a state of ecstasy to deepest despair. But what's going on inside our heads when we fall in love?

10 The American anthropologist[1] Helen Fisher describes the obsessive attachment we experience in love as 'someone camping out in your head'.

In a ground-breaking experiment, Fisher and 15 colleagues at Stony Brook University in New York state put 37 people who were madly in love into an MRI scanner. Their work showed that romantic love causes a surge of activity in brain areas that are rich in dopamine, the brain's 20 feelgood chemical.

So it's a total eclipse of the head, not the heart?

Actually...in a case of science imitating poetry, the heart has been found to influence the way we experience emotion.

25 Our brain and heart are known to be in close communication. When faced with a threat or when we spot the object of our affection in a crowded room, our heart races. But recently, scientists have turned the tables and shown 30 that feedback from our heart to our brain also influences what we are feeling.

One study, led by Prof. Sarah Garfinkel of the University of Sussex, showed that cardiovascular arousal – the bit of the heart's 35 cycle when it is working hardest – can intensify feelings of fear and anxiety. In this study, people were asked to identify scary or neutral images while their heartbeats were tracked. Garfinkel found they reacted quicker to the scary images 40 when their heart was contracting and pumping blood, compared with when it was relaxing. Her work suggests that electrical signals from blood vessels around the heart feed back into brain areas involved in emotional processing, 45 influencing how strongly we think we're feeling something.

50 Finally, in what must be a contender for one of the most romantic (or mushy) scientific insights to date, couples have been shown to have a tendency to synchronise heartbeats and breathing.

Why is it a crazy little thing?

Love is merely a madness, Shakespeare wrote. But it is only recently that scientists have offered 55 an explanation for why being in love might inspire unusual behaviour.

Donatella Marazziti, a professor of psychiatry at the University of Pisa, approached this question after carrying out research showing that people 60 with obsessive compulsive disorder have, on average, lower levels of the brain chemical serotonin in their blood. She wondered whether a similar imbalance could underlie romantic infatuation.

65 She recruited people with OCD, healthy controls and 20 people who had embarked on a romantic relationship within the previous six months. Both the OCD group and the volunteers who were in love had significantly 70 lower levels of serotonin, and the authors concluded 'that being in love literally induces a state which is not normal'. When the 'in love' group were followed up six months later, most of their serotonin levels had returned to normal.

Hannah Devlin
(Source: *Guardian* online, 11 February 2019)

Text features

Newspaper articles tend to be structured in short paragraphs, sometimes just one sentence long. The journalists want to keep the information clear, so this structure works well to get the facts across. You might notice a difference between how news is reported in print and digital media. This article was published online, so short paragraphs make it easier to scroll through and for the reader to get the gist of what is being said quickly. Newspaper articles, whether in print or online, almost always include the following features:

- a **headline** to catch the reader's attention
- a **standfirst** giving the reader a flavour of the article with the 'what, who, where and when'
- **subheadings** to break up the article, sometimes using rhetorical questions
- **connectives** to guide the reader through the different points of view
- **formal register** and vocabulary
- **quotations** from experts or witnesses giving their opinion or findings
- **statistics** and facts.

But it's not always that easy. As readers, we must use our critical thinking skills to ensure we know what point of view the article is written from. The purpose of news reporting is to inform and it should be factual, balanced and unbiased, but sometimes that is not the case and it can be persuasive and biased.

Questions

1. What 'feelgood chemical' is released when we fall in love? (1)
2. What language technique is used in 'someone camping out in your head' (lines 12–13) and why is it effective in the context of this text? (2)
3. What do you notice about the layout of the article? Why do you think it's been structured in this way? (3)
4. Who coined the phrase 'love is merely madness'? (1)
5. In your own words, explain the results of the University of Pisa OCD study. (3)

 # Language focus

To be, or not to be: that is the (rhetorical) question

Rhetorical questions are questions that do not need an answer. The answer may either be glaringly obvious, or the questioner may answer it themselves. In this case, they're used to strengthen a point. For example, 'Do you want a detention?'

Can you think of any rhetorical questions your teacher or parents have asked you? Thought so!

But rhetorical questions aren't always argumentative and can be used to create different literary effects:

- They can be used to get the reader or listener thinking.
- They're often used in persuasive writing or speeches to steer the reader or listener towards one point of view.
- As you saw in the article, they can be used as a **structural device**.

Can you think of any examples from famous pieces of writing?

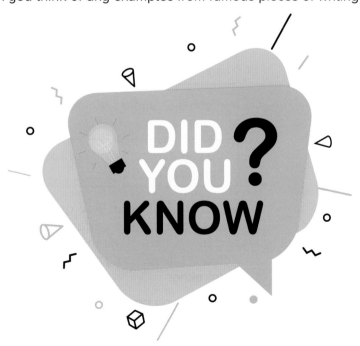

Drama focus

Work in small groups. One person should take the role of doctor. The surgery is open! One by one, the rest of the group must come into the doctor's surgery as a patient who is lovesick. They might show signs of lovesickness through a fluttering heart, inability to concentrate, lying and being secretive, butterflies in the stomach, starry eyes, head spinning or even synchronised breathing. What will the doctor prescribe?

Writing task

In this section you will write an informal letter to the speaker of 'Quickdraw', advising them and giving them recommendations. You will be focusing on **purpose**, **vocabulary**, **tone** and **form**.

With all matters of the heart, you must use your empathy skills – focus on the poem's speaker in your letter and put yourself in their shoes. The **purpose** is to give advice, so you're not telling them what to do or persuading them to do one thing in particular. You are giving them guidance and suggesting ideas by offering them options.

Vocabulary and **tone** go hand in hand. **Modal verbs** are words that indicate likelihood, whether something is certain, possible or impossible. Modal verbs are a 'softer' type of verb and provide the advisory tone we need for this letter; you would not use imperatives to advise, for example, because it wouldn't be respectful. Here are some examples that you can use in the final piece:

> *can   could   may   would   must   shall   will   should   might*

You can also show encouragement and sensitivity in your sentence starters, such as:

> *You could try...   Why not speak to...?   Perhaps you could...*
> *I suggest that...*

Watch out for **tone** in your greetings and sign off too. In a formal letter, 'Yours sincerely' is a perfect way to sign off but if you've written a letter to a friend, they might think that's a little strange! In an informal letter, you don't necessarily need to write the addresses at the top of the letter either.

The **form** you are writing in is a letter so use this writing frame to ensure you're covering all the elements required.

Your address[1]

Date[1]

Their address[1]

Dear...,[1]

1 Don't spend too long coming up with names or addresses – keep it sensible and simple!

Introduction paragraph: explain why you're writing, showing understanding of the problem, and explain roughly how you can help.

Use a paragraph for each idea or group them together if they have common themes. Give details and reasoning.

2 You are writing an informal letter so your sign off could be as simple as 'From' or 'With best wishes'. Choose a sign off which suits the writer's relationship to the recipient.

Concluding paragraph: summarise your ideas, suggest where they might find other ideas, include a closing statement.

Sign off [2] and signature.

Time to write

Now it's time to write up your finished letter. Aim for three main body paragraphs.

Imagine you are friends with the speaker of the poem 'Quickdraw'. What advice would you give them? Write a letter addressing the situation and making recommendations.

Putting pen to paper

Now have a go at one of the writing tasks below. Remember to watch out for **purpose**, **vocabulary**, **tone** and **form**.

- Write a letter to the local council making a noise complaint about your neighbours.
- Write a letter to someone you've had an argument with, either apologising or reinforcing your point.
- Write a complaint letter to a phone company.

Spelling tip: noun versus verb spellings

Check whether the word is a noun ('ice') or a verb ('ise'). *Advice* (the noun) is given when you *advise* (the verb). Still stuck? Remember that ice is a noun!

Peer review (editing/drafting)

Reviewing your writing

Swap your writing with a partner. Read each other's work carefully, looking at:

- the modal verbs they have used – are they effective?
- the way ideas are expressed – are they clear?
- how the letter is structured – do the ideas link well?

Find two positive things that would improve the writing in your view. Share these with your partner.

Edit your work, considering these changes and correcting any spelling or punctuation errors.

Wider reading

If you liked the theme of Love and heartbreak, have a look at these brilliant books:

- *We Come Apart* by Sarah Crossan and Brian Conaghan
- *Little Women* by Louisa May Alcott*
- *The Sun is Also a Star* by Nicola Yoon
- *Shakespeare's Sonnets* by William Shakespeare*
- *The Fault in Our Stars* by John Green
- *Poems to Live Your Life By* chosen by Chris Riddell
- *Pride and Prejudice* by Jane Austen*
- *Ketchup Clouds* by Annabel Pitcher
- *Troy* by Adele Geras

*Choose these titles for a more challenging read!

Book review

Prepare a short review for a book you have read recently. It might be one from the wider reading list above.

Remember to include three things about your chosen book which made you want to read on.

Share your review with a partner. What do you think of their book recommendation?

6

Inventive inventions

Aims

- **Reading focus**: Understanding character
- **Writing focus**: Narrative
- **Speaking and listening focus**: Using volume and pace
- **Language focus**: Tension devices and complex sentences
- **Drama focus**: Directing

Context

Mad scientists, bubbling test tubes and black fumes rising from a laboratory may seem a little stereotypical, but these scenarios fire up writers' imaginations. As a species we keep innovating and inventing to improve our lives. Whether it's an app to help you meditate or developing a vaccine or even an idea that might stall climate change, every invention makes a difference (good or bad).

In this chapter, we will be reading about how a great idea can turn into a disastrous one, but also how inventions can change the world for the better. You will then write a narrative full of tension, waiting to see whether an idea or invention will work out for the best or worst.

About the author

Michael Crichton (1942–2008) was an American author and filmmaker. He attended Harvard Medical School but, instead of practising as a doctor, his education influenced his writing as he created the medical drama *ER* and biotechnological franchise *Jurassic Park* from 1990.

Jurassic Park is an island theme park showcasing cloned dinosaurs. In this extract, a palaeontologist (Alan Grant), a palaeobotanist student (Ellie Sattler), a chaos theorist (Ian Malcolm) and a lawyer (Donald Gennaro) arrive at the park. Billionaire John Hammond and public relations manager, Ed Regis, show them around.

Jurassic Park

'My God,' Ellie said softly. They were all staring at the animal above the trees. *'My God.'*

Her first thought was that the dinosaur was extraordinarily beautiful. Books portrayed them as oversize, dumpy creatures, but this
5   long-necked animal had a gracefulness, almost a dignity, about its movements. And it was quick – there was nothing lumbering or dull in its behaviour. The sauropod peered alertly at them, and made a low trumpeting sound, rather like an elephant. A moment later, a second head rose above the foliage, and then a third and a fourth.

10   'My God,' Ellie said again.

Gennaro was speechless. He had known all along what to expect – he had known about it for years – but he had somehow never believed it would happen, and now, he was shocked into silence. The awesome power of the new genetic technology, which he had formerly
15   considered to be just so many words in an overwrought sales pitch – the power suddenly became clear to him. These animals were so big! They were enormous! Big as a house! And so many of them! Actual damned dinosaurs! Just as real as you could want.

Gennaro thought: We are going to make a fortune on this place. *A*
20   *fortune.*

He hoped to God the island was safe.

Grant stood on the path on the side of the hill, with the mist on his face, staring at the grey necks craning above the palms. He felt dizzy, as if the ground were sloping away too steeply. He had trouble getting his
25   breath. Because he was looking at something he had never expected to see in his life. Yet he was seeing it.

The animals in the mist were perfect apatosaurs, medium-size sauropods. His stunned mind made academic associations: North American herbivores, late Jurassic horizon. Commonly called
30 'brontosaurs.' First discovered by E.D. Cope in Montana in 1876. Specimens associated with Morrison formation strata in Colorado, Utah, and Oklahoma. Recently Berman and McIntosh had reclassified it a diplodocus based on skull appearance. Traditionally, Brontosaurus was thought to spend most of its time in shallow water, which would help
35 support its large bulk. Although this animal was clearly not in the water, it was moving much too quickly, the head and neck shifting above the palms in a very active manner – a surprisingly active manner –

Grant began to laugh.

'What is it?' Hammond said, worried. 'Is something wrong?'

40 Grant just shook its head, and continued to laugh. He couldn't tell them that what was funny was that he had seen the animal for only a few seconds, but he had already begun to accept it – and to use observations to answer long-standing questions in the field.

He was still laughing as he saw a fifth and a sixth neck crane up
45 above the palm trees. The sauropods watched the people arrive. They reminded Grant of oversize giraffes – they had the same pleasant, rather stupid gaze.

'I take it they're not animatronic,'[1] Malcom said. 'They're very lifelike.'

> **1** When a model is controlled by computers to make it move in a natural way.

'Yes, they certainly are,' Hammond said. 'Well, they should be,
50 shouldn't they?'

From the distance, they heard the trumpeting sound again. First one animal made it, and then the others joined in.

'That's their call,' Ed Regis said. 'Welcoming us to the island.'

Grant stood and listened for a moment, entranced.

55 'You probably want to know what happens next,' Hammond was saying, continuing down the path. 'We've scheduled a complete tour of the facilities for you, and a trip to see the dinosaurs in the park later this afternoon. I'll be joining you for dinner, and will answer any remaining questions you may have then. Now, if you'll go with Mr. Regis…'

60 The group followed Ed Regis toward the nearest buildings. Over the path, a crude hand-painted sign read: 'Welcome to Jurassic Park.'

Michael Crichton

Read more

The Lost World is the **sequel** to *Jurassic Park* and, as well as being a film, it's a book! If you've enjoyed a taste of the first **instalment**, try the second book too.

Questions

1 What is the definition of 'lumbering' (line 6)? (1)
2 What animal did the sauropod sound like? (1)
3 In what year and where were brontosaurs first discovered? (2)
4 Is it true that a brontosaur spends 'most of its time' in shallow water? (1) **FP**
5 What will the group be doing for the rest of the day? (3)

Punctuation focus
Complex sentences

Complex sentences are exactly how they sound: more complex than other sentences. They're usually longer, with multiple **clauses**, and generally have more punctuation within them. Here's an example:

The sauropod peered alertly at them, and made a low trumpeting sound, rather like an elephant.

You could remove the subordinate clause from the middle and the sentence would still make sense, but that extra information makes it complex.

It can be useful to think of sentences like a train. They're made of different carriages (clauses) which are connected (by **conjunctions** or punctuation). They also start at a station (capital letter) and end at a station (full stop). Complex sentences are just longer trains, carrying more cargo (information)!

Context

The Age of Enlightenment: During the seventeenth and eighteenth centuries in Europe, philosophers and scientists began sharing more of their ideas with a wider audience. Reasoning and logic were the order of the day, which led to the questioning of long-held religious beliefs. The Shelleys wrote with hindsight about this seismic shift in thinking in their novels and poems, reflecting on its insights and limitations.

About the author

Mary Wollstonecraft Shelley (1797–1851) was an English novelist. At aged just 19, she married the poet Percy Bysshe Shelley following a scandalous affair. She remained a political radical throughout her life but for over a century her own writing remained in the shadow of her husband's.

Frankenstein is considered to be one of the first Gothic novels. It was first published anonymously in 1818 when Mary Shelley was only 20. A young scientist, Victor Frankenstein, creates a humanoid by assembling parts from different dead bodies. Despite Victor working for years to achieve this and selecting the most beautiful parts, he is repulsed by his creation.

Frankenstein

It was on a dreary night of November, that I beheld the accomplishment of my toils. With an anxiety that almost amounted to agony, I collected the instruments of life around me,
5 that I might infuse a spark of being into the lifeless thing that lay at my feet. It was already one in the morning; the rain pattered dismally against the panes, and my candle was nearly burnt out, when, by the glimmer of the half-
10 extinguished light, I saw the dull yellow eye of the creature open; it breathed hard, and a convulsive motion agitated its limbs.

How can I describe my emotions at this catastrophe, or how delineate the wretch

15 whom with such infinite pains and care I had endeavoured to form? His limbs were in proportion, and I had selected his features as beautiful. Beautiful! – Great God! His yellow skin scarcely covered the work of muscles and
20 arteries beneath; his hair was of a lustrous black, and flowing; his teeth of a pearly whiteness; but these luxuriances only formed a more horrid contrast with his watery eyes, that seemed almost of the same colour as the
25 dun white sockets in which they were set, his shrivelled complexion and straight black lips. The different accidents of life are not so changeable as the feelings of human nature. I

had worked hard for nearly two years, for the
30 sole purpose of infusing life into an inanimate
body. For this I had deprived myself of rest
and health. I had desired it with an ardour that
far exceeded moderation; but now that I had
finished, the beauty of the dream vanished,
35 and breathless horror and disgust filled my
heart. Unable to endure the aspect of the being
I had created, I rushed out of the room, and
continued a long time traversing my bed-
chamber, unable to compose my mind to sleep.
40 At length lassitude[1] succeeded to the tumult
I had before endured; and I threw myself on
the bed in my clothes, endeavouring to seek
a few moments of forgetfulness. But it was in
vain: I slept, indeed, but I was disturbed by
45 the wildest dreams. I thought I saw Elizabeth,
in the bloom of health, walking in the streets

of Ingolstadt. Delighted and surprised, I
embraced her; but as I imprinted the first kiss
on her lips, they became livid with the hue of
50 death; her features appeared to change, and I
thought I held the corpse of my dead mother
in my arms; a shroud enveloping her form, and
I saw the graveworms crawling in the folds of
the flannel. I started from my sleep in horror;
55 a cold dew covered my forehead, my teeth
chattered, and every limb became convulsed:
when, by the dim and yellow light of the
moon, as it forced its way through the window
shutters, I beheld the wretch – the miserable
60 monster whom I had created. He held up the
curtain of the bed; and his eyes, if eyes they
may be called, were fixed on me. His jaws
opened, and he muttered some inarticulate
sounds, while a grin wrinkled his cheeks. He
65 might have spoken, but I did not hear; one
hand was stretched out, seemingly to detain
me, but I escaped, and rushed downstairs. I
took refuge in the courtyard belonging to the
house which I inhabited; where I remained
70 during the rest of the night, walking up and
down in the greatest agitation, listening
attentively, catching and fearing each sound
as if it were to announce the approach of the
demonical corpse to which I had so miserably
75 given life.

Mary Wollstonecraft Shelley

1 A weariness of body
and mind; lacking
energy.

Questions

1 What time of year is it? (1)
2 It is 6pm. True or false? (1) **FP**
3 In the context of the passage, what does 'agitated' mean (line 12)? (1)
4 What is the definition of 'ardour' (line 32)? (1)
5 What 'forced its way through the window shutters'? (1)

Punctuation tip: ellipsis

Ellipsis is useful to add tension or suspense to your creative writing but
only...if it's not overused. For example:

But what I heard next made my blood run cold...

Remember it is made of only three dots too!

Research

The nineteenth century saw some rapid technological change but not everyone reacted positively. The speed of the changes made many in the religious society concerned and you can see that concern reflected in the literature of the time. But what changes were occurring?

Take some time to research the following areas and how they evolved during the nineteenth century:

- the building of the railways
- medicine
- fingerprinting in policing
- the Industrial Revolution
- Darwinism and evolutionary theory.

Talking point

In small groups, discuss the following question:

In what ways do scientific advancements, such as medical discoveries, communication and entertainment devices or public transportation, affect society?

You may want to base your discussion around the following areas:

- education
- work/leisure
- family life
- equality.

Writing questions on *Jurassic Park*

1 Looking at the whole extract, what is effective about the structure? (3)
2 What is your impression of Gennaro? (4)
3 What is your impression of Grant? (4)

Writing questions on *Frankenstein*

1 How does the description of the weather add to the atmosphere of the extract? (4)
2 What is implied by Frankenstein's vivid dreams? (4)
3 In your opinion, what wakes Frankenstein? Refer closely to the text to support your answer. (3)

Speaking and listening focus
Volume and pace in storytelling

Altering your volume and pace are a great way of creating tension when telling a story. Just think of scary movies or TV shows you have watched – the music always builds to a crescendo when there's a chase and there is always silence just before a **jump scare**. You can recreate that by the way you read.

Read the *Frankenstein* extract from line 31 until the end out loud to a partner. Experiment with volume and pace. When is it effective? When is it not? Try to achieve the perfect balance to create the most tension possible.

Punctuation tip

Listing can be an effective writing feature, but the commas have to be in the correct places. Put a **comma** between single items in a list but use an 'and' between the final two items. For example:

I would like the pasta, pizza and pastrami.

Occasionally, you *can* use a comma before an 'and'. This is called an Oxford comma but is usually only used for clarity or stylistically. For example:

I love my friends, London and Paris (are your friends called London and Paris?).

I love my friends, London, and Paris (I see you love the cities as well as your friends).

For how to use **semicolons** in lists, look at page 78 in Love and heartbreak.

Thematic focus

Even though the characters in the extracts above had dreamed of the moment of seeing the creations come to fruition, they all react in different ways.

Fill in the table below with adjectives which describe their contrasting reactions. Look at their actions, dialogue and the descriptions of them to help you.

Extract 1: *Jurassic Park*	Extract 2: *Frankenstein*
disbelief	shock
excitement	terror
awe	panic

Extended writing questions

You will now be writing an extended answer about an extract. Write your answer in three PEEA paragraphs, using evidence from the text to support your ideas. (See page 179 in the Exam skills chapter for an explanation of the PEEA technique.)

Here are some tips for writing extended answers:

- Read the questions carefully.
- Use the three foci in your topic sentences for the three paragraphs.
- It might help you to find your evidence for each before you start writing.
- Use connectives like 'and', 'furthermore', 'however' and 'additionally' to expand your explanations.

1 How does the author show the difference in the characters through their reactions in Extract 1?

Make sure that you discuss tone, language and vocabulary.

OR

2 How is tension created by the author in Extract 2?

Consider sentence structure, vocabulary and description.

OR

3 Write a diary entry from the perspective of one of the characters in either extract, explaining the important event that features in the extract:
- what happened that was significant that day
- their thoughts and feelings about it
- what they think will happen now.

About the author

Robert Louis Stevenson wrote the novella *The Strange Case of Dr Jekyll and Mr Hyde* in 1886. It tells the story of a lawyer trying to untangle the connection between his old friend, Dr Jekyll, and an evil Mr Edward Hyde. Little does he know that they're one and the same, created in Dr Jekyll's own laboratory.

Evan Placey reimagined the novel in play form for the National Youth Theatre (2017). In his version, Victorian London collides with the present day and it is Jekyll's widow, Harriet, that makes the breakthrough in the laboratory. In the first scene, Harriet Jekyll asks the Royal Society of Scientists for support to continue her late husband's work.

Jekyll and Hyde

JEKYLL	I'm asking to become a Fellow of the Society.
	I know it is perhaps unorthodox.
	But I need something to keep me occupied.
	And I want desperately to carry on this work.
5	I am asking you to take a leap of faith.
LANYON	It is because you are grieving and because of Henry's standing in this Society that we have given you ear this afternoon. As a courtesy. And I tried to dissuade you of this path to save you embarrassment.
10	And then you suggest to this council – doctors who have studied for years – that you, a woman who has not so much as filled a beaker with water, will simply, what, get down to it. You insult this council, and so I will not spare you by officially considering your request.
15	Mrs Harriet Jekyll would like to be nominated to the council. All those in favour say 'Aye'.

Silence.

	Well, there you have it.
	We recognise you are looking for something to keep you occupied.
20	
	May I suggest you take up needlework. Or some such thing appropriate to your skills.

Scene Eight

The Laboratory

25 ABBIE	Madam? Is everything alright? You didn't have any dinner.
	ABBIE sees JEKYLL has been crying. Gets her a cloth.
JEKYLL	You've always been good to me, Abbie.
	Do you like it here?
ABBIE	I am very thankful to you and Mr Jekyll.
30 JEKYLL	I didn't ask if you were thankful.
	I asked if you liked it here.

Beat.

ABBIE	Of course.
JEKYLL	Not 'of course'. I can't imagine what there is to like.
35 ABBIE	Is everything okay, my lady? Shall I bring up some tea?
JEKYLL	No, thank you. I don't want to be disturbed for the rest of the evening.
ABBIE	Certainly, my lady. *[Exits]*

40 *JEKYLL suddenly springs up. With renewed determination, she measures out powders, liquids, lets them boil and smoke together.*

[JEKYLL takes the potion she has made and waits for it to take effect…]

… Nothing.

Disappointment. Giving up. And then suddenly:

Her body contorts. Is pulled. She's still JEKYLL but it's like something inside
45 *is trying to get out. She's thrown against her equipment, scattering and smashing things. She's fighting to keep hold of her body. With each pull/contortion, a woman's silhouette appears in the mirror in a pose of seduction, anarchy, freedom. So that the silhouettes are all around her. Before us, JEKYLL TRANFORMS.*

50 *And standing before us is HYDE. And she ain't the monster we're expecting. She stands taller, more confident than her alter-ego. This is a woman who makes heads turn.*

Beat.

She notices a broken nail from the ordeal. She pulls off the hanging nail
55 *with her teeth.*

HYDE Dammit, I only did these yesterday.

What? What you starin' at? Ain't none of you ever had a broken nail before?

And now we realise 'we' are another mirror. She applies bright lipstick.
60 *Grabs an umbrella. Eyes herself up.*

Lady Hyde has arrived.

Evan Placey

Questions

1 What is the definition of 'unorthodox' (line 2)? (1)

2 What does Lanyon suggest Jekyll take up instead of scientific work? (1)

3 What does Hyde do before she notices the audience? (1)

4 Which adjective best describes Lady Hyde? (1)
   a confident
   b petty
   c arrogant
   d introverted **FP**

Extended writing questions

You will now be writing an extended answer to the question below. Write your answer in three PEEA paragraphs, using evidence from the text to support your ideas. (See page 179 in the Exam skills for an explanation of the PEEA technique.)

Here are some tips for writing extended answers:

● Read the questions carefully.
● Use the three foci in your topic sentences for the three paragraphs.
● It might help you to find your evidence for each before you start writing.
● Use connectives 'and', 'furthermore', 'however' and 'additionally' to expand your explanations.

How does the playwright, Evan Placey, make these scenes entertaining and thought-provoking?

Consider these three points:

● the presentation of Harriet Jekyll in each scene
● dramatic effects, including the use of props and physical theatre
● what the scenes suggest about the reasons why Harriet Jekyll tries to transform.

Text features

Aspects of the Gothic

Frankenstein is considered one of the first Gothic novels but *Jekyll and Hyde* also contains many Gothic elements. The Gothic is so ingrained in our popular culture that we barely notice it, but at the time it was a huge innovation. You may also have heard of it through Gothic architecture or art. Watch out for these Gothic literary conventions:

- fear and uneasiness
- mysterious atmosphere
- a mixture of horror and romance
- omens or curses
- creepy settings
- supernatural activity
- anti-heroes and villains
- nightmares
- emotional distress.

In the play extract, Lady Hyde talks to the audience (which is called 'breaking the fourth wall'). This adds to the sense of uneasiness because the playwright removes her from the action to talk directly to us.

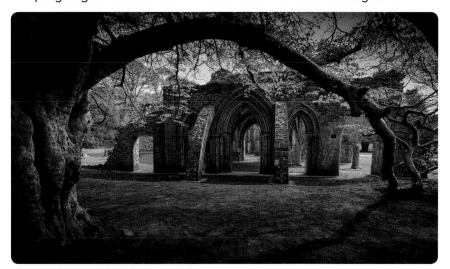

Language focus

Pathetic fallacy

Another way of creating an atmosphere worthy of the Gothic is by using **pathetic fallacy**. Pathetic fallacy is when the weather described indicates a character's mood. For example:

the rain pattered dismally against the panes

This quotation, particularly the personification of the rain's falling as 'dismally', suggests Victor Frankenstein's anxiety about creating life and that he is not as excited or enthused about this as perhaps he should be.

It can also **foreshadow** an event. A storm rarely happens in a book just before something good occurs.

And, of course, it creates atmosphere. A good tip if you have trouble starting pieces of creative writing is to describe the weather. That will set the mood for the whole piece.

Writing questions in *Jekyll and Hyde*

1. How does the structure of the second scene make the transformation more dramatic? (3)
2. How is Hyde different to Jekyll? Explain your answer using evidence from the text. (4)
3. What is the effect of having Hyde talk directly to the audience? (3)

Context

The Science Museum in London is an amazing resource for discovering the origin of both ordinary and extraordinary inventions. Its exhibitions feature scientific, technological and medical advancements from across the globe.

This extract is part of a longer feature about the humble vacuum cleaner on the museum's website. You can read the whole piece alongside other stories about the invention of everyday technologies, such as the lightbulb and the kettle.

1   A 64-metre-high Ferris wheel in Prater amusement park, Vienna.

2   Dressed in the special uniform of the company.

'The invention of the vacuum cleaner, from horse-drawn to high tech'

THE INVENTION OF THE VACUUM CLEANER

In 1901, if you were lucky, you might have witnessed a startling scene on the streets of London—one which would quickly revolutionise how most of us clean our homes.

5   Engineer Hubert Cecil Booth was rolling his new vacuum cleaner onto the wealthier streets of town.

First employed by Maudslay, Sons and Field in Lambeth in the 1890s, at the time he was better known for designing suspension bridges and fairground Ferris wheels (including Vienna's famous Riesenrad[1]).

10   But in 1901 he turned his skill to carpet cleaning after witnessing the demonstration of a new machine at London's Empire Music Hall.

He realised that the machine on display had a fatal flaw. It was designed to blow out air in the hope of raising the dust from the carpet and into the collecting bag. The inventor told him that the method Booth suggested
15   instead—sucking up the dirt through a filter—was impossible.

Challenge accepted, Booth set off on a mission to produce a machine that would suck, not blow.

After allegedly near-fatal tests—in which he choked after putting a handkerchief 'filter' over his mouth and sucking up dust from the arm
20   of a chair—Booth formed the British Vacuum Cleaner Company and launched his new device. This was the huge beast of a machine seen doing the rounds of wealthy Londoners' homes at the start of the twentieth century.

THE FIRST VACUUM CLEANER IN ACTION

25   Channelling a red and gold fire engine aesthetic, according to journalist and author Jane Furnival, the distinctive horse-drawn vacuum cleaner and its liveried[2] operators arrived at your house, immediately advertising to the neighbourhood that you were holding a 'vacuum tea party'. A visit wasn't cheap—the cost was the same as the annual wages of a 'tweeny', a
30   junior domestic maid.

To conduct the miraculous cleaning, long hoses were fed through windows, the petrol-powered motor (and later electric engine) was started and air was drawn by suction from the hose and nozzles through a filter.

35   Locals outside were encouraged to marvel at the amount of dirt and dust collected through a special glass chamber on the side of the machine— another cunning marketing strategy.

VACUUM CLEANING AS A LUXURY

40 After a flurry of disapproval and a string of court cases, both against the disruption the machine caused on the streets (including frightening horses) and from a series of disgruntled inventors, Booth finally convinced judge and jury that his powerful machine was the only vacuum cleaner at the time that actually worked.

Cleaning everywhere from Buckingham Palace to the Royal Mint and
45 Crystal Palace – where 26 tons of dust were removed from the girders during a First World War outbreak of spotted fever – its credentials were soon established as a reliable cleaning machine.

Vacuum cleaners were purchased by Russia's Tzar Nicholas II, Germany's Kaiser Wilhelm II, the House of Commons and the popular
50 Dickens & Jones department store in London.

Despite the drama and theatre of Booth's machine, the basic technology and the suction principle was the same as in most vacuum cleaners today.

(Source: Science Museum)

Questions

1 In what year did Booth start creating and testing his new vacuum cleaner? (1)
2 What was Booth most famous for designing before the vacuum cleaner? (2)
3 Booth almost choked when testing a vacuum cleaner. True or false? (1) **FP**
4 What is your impression of Booth? (4)
5 In your own words, explain how Booth's invention was successful. (3)

Text features

Online texts

When writing an online feature, it's important to stick to short, impactful paragraphs. If you compare the last extract to the first two, you will see how different the lengths of paragraphs are. Shorter paragraphs make it easier for a reader to scroll through and for a web designer to format.

Due to the brevity of the paragraphs, the writer has had to jam in as much information as possible. They often use adverbial phrases to start sentences to achieve this. For example:

Channelling a red and gold fire engine aesthetic...

After a flurry of disapproval and a string of court cases...

These are written creatively and make the piece engaging. Even though it seems good online feature writing must be brief, it certainly isn't boring!

For more information on web articles, look back at page 37 in the Our planet chapter.

Language focus

Devices to create tension

If any of Booth's story had been written as a narrative, it would definitely use devices to create tension. Here are some possible examples:

- Complex sentences, which delay the action by adding description:
  Slowly and carefully, Booth and his team fed the long, dark hose through the upper window of the townhouse, which stood on the grandest of avenues overlooking St James' Park.
- Short sentences which create tension:
  Challenge completed.
- Onomatopoeia or no sound at all:
  There was a heavy silence from the onlookers before a slow and steady booming as the dust filled the glass chamber.
- Ambiguity – consider the use of the pronoun 'it' and metaphorical comparisons:
  It trundled down the road, an elephant emblazoned with red and gold lettering ready for the watering hole, but in this case the water would be pure dust.

Drama focus

In groups of four, decide who will be the three actors and the one director. The actors should read through the extract from *Jekyll and Hyde* without any expression. The director should then give them advice about how to say certain lines to create two distinctive characters. Do a second reading, taking on this advice. The director should give more feedback, constantly developing the characters. When you're ready, add guidance on movement (**blocking**) to bring it to life!

Writing task

You are going to write a narrative full of tension entitled 'It worked!' The narrative will be about someone who had a brilliant idea or created an invention. But will it work out for the best or the worst?

Use the planning frame below to help you structure your tense narrative:

First paragraph

Set the scene – describe the weather, atmospheric setting, set the mood.

Second paragraph

Build-up – use those tension devices to delay the event, lots of description, silence.

Third paragraph

The event – it worked! What sounds does it make?

Fourth paragraph

The twist – this could just be one sentence that turns everything on its head.

Time to write

Write a narrative entitled 'It worked!' about an idea or invention.

Putting pen to paper

Now try one of the writing tasks below, employing tension devices:

1   Write a short story about Halloween.
2   Write a narrative that features the line, 'Well, I didn't know that would happen.'
3   Write a short story with the title, 'The Ruin'.

Spelling tip: -full or -ful

Only use 'full' when full, for example: *full up, full marks.*
Use 'ful' when you're adding to a word, for example: *wonderful, powerful.*

Peer review (editing/drafting)

Reviewing your writing

Swap your piece of narrative writing with a partner. Read each other's work carefully, looking at:

- any tension devices you spot – have they been used effectively?
- the way ideas/points of view are expressed – are they clear?
- how the narrative is structured – do the ideas link well?

Find two positive things that would improve the writing in your view. Share these with your partner.

Edit your work, considering these changes and correcting any spelling or punctuation errors.

Wider reading

Hungry for more fantastical created worlds and imaginative inventions? Have a look at these brilliant books:

- *Mortal Engines* by Philip Reeve*
- *Cogheart* by Peter Bunzl
- *The Hound of the Baskervilles* by Sir Arthur Conan Doyle*
- *His Dark Materials* by Philip Pullman
- *Brightstorm* by Vashti Hardy
- *The Time Machine* by H.G. Wells*

*Choose these titles for a more challenging read!

Book review

Draw a diagram of an invention or magical object from a book you've read. It could even be from the wider reading list above. Make sure you label it.

Ask a partner to ask you questions about your diagram. What does it reveal about the plot and characters of the book? Does it make them want to read the book?

7 New kids

Aims

- **Reading focus**: Inferring information about characters
- **Writing focus**: Descriptive narrative
- **Speaking and listening focus**: Open and closed questions; interviewing
- **Language focus**: Structure and metre, the active and the passive voice
- **Drama focus**: Monologues

Context

There are more than 25 million refugees worldwide and more than 11 million of them are child refugees. Refugees are people who are fleeing their own countries because of violence, natural disasters or war. They are often seeking refuge from terrible situations, leaving behind their homes, possessions and loved ones, but they do carry hope with them.

In this chapter, you will meet refugees at different stages of their journey to safety. One is stuck in a detention centre, the other has just arrived as the new kid at school, and the last has made a name for himself in politics since arriving in the UK as a child refugee. You'll also read some poetry which addresses the treatment of refugees. Finally, you'll use all that you have learnt to write a description of the first day at a new school in role as the 'new kid'.

About the author

Zana Fraillon is an Australian multi-award-winning author. She undertakes careful research for all her books, which was rewarded when *The Bone Sparrow* (2016) won the Amnesty CILIP Honour Award.

Subhi is a refugee from Myanmar, living in a modern-day Australian detention centre. It is all he has ever known but his hopeful nature shines through. In this extract, we are introduced to his family and their living conditions.

The Bone Sparrow

Sometimes, at night, the dirt outside turns into a beautiful ocean. As red as the sun and as deep as the sky.

I lie on the bed, Queeny's feet pushing against my cheek, and listen to the waves lapping at the tent. Queeny says I'm stupid, saying that kind

5 of stuff. But it's true. She doesn't see it, is all. Our maá says there are some people in this world who can see all the hidden bits and pieces of the universe blown in on the north wind and scattered about in the shadows. Queeny, she never tries to look in the shadows. She doesn't even squint.

10 Maá sees, though. She can hear the ocean outside too. 'You hear it, né?' I whisper, my fingers feeling for her smile in the dark.

In the morning, the ground still wet and foamy from where those waves washed up, I sit and trace the hundreds of animals that have swum all the way up to the tent, their faces pushing against the flaps,

15 trying to get a look at us inside our beds. Queeny says they aren't real beds, but just old army cots and even older army blankets. Queeny says that a real bed is made with springs and cushions and feathers, and that real blankets don't itch.

I don't think those animals would know the difference or really care

20 much either.

This morning I found a shell washed up right along with those animals. I breathed in its smell. All hot and salty fish, like the very bottom of the ocean. And even though Queeny doesn't believe, and grunted about when was I ever going to grow up and could I please quit bothering her

25 all the goddamn time, she still gave me her last bit of paper and said I could borrow her pen so I could write the words in black at the top of the page. The Night Sea With Creatures. I drew a picture as best I could with no colours and paper that curled from the damp. Using her pen and paper only cost me my soap, and I'll steal that back from her later

30 anyway. Sisters shouldn't charge their own brothers for paper.

I snug up to Maá, my legs curled up in hers – but careful not to wake her because today is one of her tired days – and look through all the pictures in my box. I'll need to find a new box soon. The rats have eaten most of one side, and what's left is wet and mouldy, even after I
35 left it out in the sun to dry. There are some pictures down the bottom that are headed with Maá's writing from way back, before I could write on my own. I like Maá's writing more. When she writes, it's like the words seep out on to the page already perfect. I push my fingers over Maá's letters, breathing them in like the smells from my shell.

40 Tomorrow, when she's better, I'll show Maá my new picture, and the shell, and tell her again about the Night Sea and its treasures. I'll tell her every little bit and listen to her laugh and watch her smile.

When I untangle my legs and whisper that it's just about breakfast time and does she want to come eat, I see her eyes open a bit and the smile
45 start on her lips. 'Just a little longer, né?' she says, in her English that never sounds right. 'I not hungry, Subhi, love.'

Maá's never hungry much. The last time she ate a full meal and didn't just peck at her food was when I was only nineteen fence diamonds high. I remember because that was on Queeny's birthday and Maá
50 always measures us on our birthdays. By now I am least twenty-one or twenty-two, or maybe even twenty-two and a half high. I haven't been measured in a while.

Maá's never hungry much, but I'm always hungry.

Zana Fraillon

Read more

Refugee Boy (2015) by Benjamin Zephaniah relates the story of Alem, a boy from war-torn Ethiopia, who finds himself left alone in London, seeking refugee status as his parents believe this will be the safest option for him.

Questions

1 Who is Maá? (1)
2 What did Subhi trade for pen and paper? (1)
3 What has been eating the box? (1)
4 On what day are their heights always measured? (1)

Grammar focus
Active and passive voice

Sentences can be described as active or passive. We can choose to write in an active or passive voice depending on what effect we want to create.

In the **active voice**, the **subject** is doing the action. For example:

I found a shell washed up.

The active voice is used for more informal writing and it feels more personal.

In the **passive voice**, the object is having the action done to it. For example:

A shell was found washed up.

The passive voice is used for more formal writing and it has the effect of objectivity. It also removes the subject from the sentence, making it hard to say who is to blame for an action. For example:

The government has not addressed the views of refugees. (active voice)

becomes

The views of refugees have not been addressed. (passive voice)

For more about **voice**, see page 33 in the Our planet chapter.

About the author

Onjali Q Rauf is a British author and founder of an NGO called Making Herstory. Her work is in part influenced by her experiences with racism as a child. *The Boy at the Back of the Class* (2018) is about a refugee child who has just arrived in Britain and was inspired by real life refugees Rauf met in a Calais refugee camp.

In the extract, the narrator (a child himself) recounts how the 'new boy' plays football with some classmates, but not all his classmates are as welcoming.

The Boy at the Back of the Class

When the bell rung for first break the next morning, Mrs Khan kept her promise and let the new boy out into the playground for the very first time. Tom was put in charge of looking after

5 him and we were all told that if he got scared or wanted to stop playing, then we were to find a teacher immediately or go and see Ms Hemsi in the staff room. I didn't know why the new boy would be scared of being in the playground, or

10 why he wouldn't want to play with us, but then I thought that maybe in his country, the bullies had been mean to him at school too. I'd never really thought about it before, but maybe there are bullies in everyone's playground.

15 As Josie grabbed her football, Tom tried to explain to the new boy how to play the game properly.

'You! Like THIS!' said Tom loudly, pointing to the new boy, then his foot and then the ball.

The new boy nodded.

20 'But NOT like THIS!' continued Tom, shaking his head before pointing to the football and then his hand.

'This is stupid! He *knows* how to play football!' said Michael.

25 'Maybe they play it differently in his country. Remember when I got here and I only knew American football?' protested Tom, looking at me as if I knew the answer.

I shrugged. 'I don't know! We should have
30 asked Ms Hemsi!'

'Oh, come *on*!' cried Josie as we reached the playground. 'Let's just let him try and see if he knows it.'

By the time we had reached our usual corner of
35 the playground, Josie and Tom had decided that the new boy would be on Josie and Michael's team. Since she was the best at football, it wouldn't matter so much if the new boy couldn't play. And because it was just Tom and
40 me on my team, we had the first kick.

After less than a minute of the game starting, the new boy began to run and dribble and do lots of tricks with the football that none of us could do yet. And within the first five minutes,
45 he had scored two goals.

'Whoah!' said Tom. 'He's even better than Josie!' Suddenly catching Josie's eye, he quickly added, 'Or nearly as good, anyway!'

'Wooooohoooooo!' cried out Michael as the
50 new boy flashed past me and Tom and struck another goal. 'Wooooohoooooo!'

By now, a crowd was beginning to gather to watch the game, and I could hear lots of upper graders and lower graders talking and saying
55 things like, 'Look! The dangerous kid's been allowed out!' and 'Does this mean he doesn't have a disease?' and 'But the kidnappers will be able to see him from here!'

I had just heard Jennie tell everyone that she
60 was sure she had heard Mrs Sanders say the new boy was a professional footballer, when she suddenly cried out 'OOOOWWWWW!' and before we knew what was happening, Brendan-the-Bully and his mates, Liam and Chris, had
65 pushed their way onto our make-believe pitch.

Josie looked at me and I looked at Tom, and Tom looked over at the new boy, who was standing next to Michael looking confused.

'We want to play,' said Brendan-the-Bully, a
70 nasty smile on his face. He walked over to the new boy, who had the football, and kicked the ball away so hard that it ended up on the other side of the playground. The new boy took a step back.

75 'Go away, Brendan,' said Josie, bravely. 'This is our game and that's MY ball!'

Brendan-the-Bully turned around to look at Josie, and she swallowed nervously. But just then his expression changed from mean to sad.

80 I turned around too and saw that Mr Irons was walking towards us.

'What's going on here then?' he asked, his moustache twitching.

Onjali Q Rauf

Questions

1 Who is on the new boy's football team? (1)
   a Tom and Josie
   b Brendan and Liam
   c Liam and Chris
   d Josie and Michael **FP**
2 Who is the best at football? (1)
3 How many goals does the new boy score in the first five minutes? (1)
4 What are the names of Brendan-the-Bully's mates? (2)

Punctuation tip: time for a comma

If you start a sentence with an adverb or adverbial phrase, remember your comma. You automatically pause after one when you read it, so that's a good way to check. For example:

Cautiously,[1] *he picked up the ball.* ← | 1 Adverb + comma |

Later that day,[2] *they played football again.* | 2 Adverbial phrase + comma |

The worldwide refugee crisis is ongoing. If you want to find out the latest information, here are some organisations to look up who offer fantastic resources and ways to help:

- Save the Children
- UNHCR
- Kiddle
- Children's Society

Talking point

Imagine a new pupil starts at your school and they are from another country. Discuss in small groups how you would help them feel welcome. Here are some things to think about:

- school rules
- breaks and lunchtimes
- religious beliefs and routines
- subjects you study.

Writing questions on *The Bone Sparrow*

1 Who is Queeny and how can you tell? (2)
2 How does the author create a vivid image of the family's living conditions? (4)
3 What do you think is wrong with Maá? Refer closely to the text in your answer. (2)
4 This is the opening of the book. In what three ways is it effective? (3)

Writing questions on *The Boy at the Back of the Class*

1 How does the reader know the new boy is good at football? (4)
2 How do the characters' reactions to Brendan suggest that he is a bully? (4)
3 Have the children been told about the new boy's background? How can you tell? (3)
4 Choose two characters from the extract. What is your impression of them? (4)

Speaking and listening focus
Interviewing

Some interviews that you listen to or read seem to flow like a conversation. Others can be more stilted. That can be down to the choice of questions.

Closed questions only require a 'yes' or 'no' or brief answers. For example, 'Do you like apples?'

Open questions allow the interviewee to give longer answers. For example, 'What is your first memory of apples?'

As an interviewer, you should base your questions around the answers you hope to get.

Write a set of questions for a partner to discover what they know from the news about refugees. Make sure you have a balance of open and closed questions. See how they respond differently to different questions.

Thematic focus

The two extracts feature refugees at different stages of their journeys: Subhi is in a detention centre and the new boy is in a school in a new country. Even though they are told from different points of view, as readers we can see how they are both reacting to their situations. Consider and compare their reactions to their current situations.

Select the best words from the list below to inspire your comparisons:

- angry
- content
- coping
- defensive
- desperate
- hopeful
- optimistic
- persevering.

Write a paragraph putting forward your comparative points.

Extended writing questions

You will now be writing an extended answer about an extract. Write your answer in three PEEA paragraphs, using evidence from the text to support your ideas. (See page 179 in the Exam skills chapter for an explanation of the PEEA technique.)

Here are some tips for writing extended answers:

- Read the questions carefully.
- Use the three foci in your topic sentences for the three paragraphs.
- It might help you to find your evidence for each before you start writing.
- Use connectives like 'and', 'furthermore', 'however' and 'additionally' to expand your explanations.

1 Subhi is an optimistic and hopeful character in *The Bone Sparrow*. How can you tell this from Extract 1?

   Focus on his actions, his thoughts and description.

OR

2 How do the classmates of the new boy in Extract 2 show him consideration?

   Focus on their actions, their dialogue and the narrative perspective.

OR

3 Write the new boy's diary entry that evening. You should explain what happened during breaktime, how he feels when he plays football and how others react to him.

About the author

Brian Bilston is often called the Poet Laureate of Instagram, but he has never revealed his true identity. He writes almost every day in all forms of poetry and manages to write what we're all thinking in that moment with a dose of humour. As well as capturing the zeitgeist (the 'spirit of the age'), he also writes about serious subjects, as this poem from 2016 shows.

'Refugees'

They have no need of our help

So do not tell me

These haggard faces could belong to you or me

Should life have dealt a different hand[1]

We need to see them for who they really are

Chancers and scroungers

Layabouts and loungers

With bombs up their sleeves

Cut-throats and thieves[2]

They are not

Welcome here

We should make them

Go back to where they came from[3]

They cannot

Share our food

Share our homes

Share our countries[4]

Instead let us

Build a wall to keep them out[5]

It is not okay to say

These are people just like us

A place should only belong to those who are born there

Do not be so stupid to think that

The world can be looked at another way

(now read from bottom to top)[6]

Brian Bilston

1   Personification here enhances the feel of luck and chance. We could be in their position.

2   A rhyme scheme emerges briefly in these four lines to create rhythm for either order.

3   A stereotypical phrase made more potent by the lines that surround it.

4   Repetition creates rhythm and emphasis.

5   This imperative phrase became 'popularised' during the US presidential election in 2016.

6   The instructions come at the end to surprise us. It leaves the reader with the positive version too.

Language focus
Palindromes

Palindromes are a sequence of letters, words, phrases or numbers that can be read backwards and forwards. The word itself comes from Greek root words for 'again' (*palin*) and 'running' (*dromos*).

You can have single-word palindromes, like 'madam', 'racecar' or 'Hannah', that go letter by letter. But it gets little more complex when you use whole words, and the sentence must make sense when read one way and then read backwards. For example, 'Was it a car or a cat I saw?'

Poets create longer palindromes (sometimes known as mirrored poetry) where whole verses can be read forwards and backwards and still make sense. That's when punctuation becomes very tricky!

They're difficult to write but a fun challenge too. Now that you have read the poem, have a go yourself!

Research

Palindromes are just like puzzles! Here are some tasks to get you puzzling over palindromes:

- What famous palindromes are there? Search for these.
- How are palindromes used in music? Ask your Music teacher to help if you're stuck.
- Is there anyone in your school with a name palindrome?
- How many palindromic numbers can you come up with? Ask your Maths teacher to check them.

1 Merciful.

Speech from *Sir Thomas More*

Grant them removed, and grant that this your noise

Hath chid down all the majesty of England;

Imagine that you see the wretched strangers,

Their babies at their backs and their poor luggage,

5 Plodding to the ports and coasts for transportation,

And that you sit as kings in your desires,

Authority quite silenced by your brawl,

And you in ruff of your opinions clothed;

What had you got? I'll tell you: you had taught

10 How insolence and strong hand should prevail,

How order should be quelled; and by this pattern

Not one of you should live an aged man,

For other ruffians, as their fancies wrought,

With self-same hand, self-reason, and self-right,

15 Would shark on you, and men like ravenous fishes

Feed on one another. [...] Alas, alas, say now the King,

As he is clement[1] if th'offender mourn,

Should so much come too short of your great trespass

As but to banish you: whither would you go?

20 What country, by the nature of your error,

Should give you harbour? Go you to France or Flanders,

To any German province, to Spain or Portugal,

Nay, anywhere that not adheres to England,

Why, you must needs be strangers. Would you be pleas'd

25 To find a nation of such barbarous temper

That breaking out in hideous violence

Would not afford you an abode on earth.

Whet their detested knives against your throats,

Spurn you like dogs, and like as if that God

30 Owned not nor made not you, nor that the elements

Were not all appropriate to your comforts,

But charter'd unto them? What would you think

To be thus used? This is the strangers' case

And this your mountainish inhumanity.

William Shakespeare

Questions

1 What are the 'wretched strangers' carrying (line 3)? (2)
2 What language technique is used in 'you sit as kings in your desires' (line 6)? (1)
3 What does the phrase 'Not one of you should live an aged man' mean? (line 12) (1)
4 What is the definition of 'barbarous'? (line 25) (1)

Text features

Poetic meter

Meter is another term for rhythm. Meter is measured in syllables or iambs (two syllables) which are called 'feet'. Iambic pentameter is type of metric line made up of 10 syllables, five of which are stressed and five unstressed. For example:

*To / **be** / thus / **used**? / This / **is** / the / **stran**/gers' / **case**.*

Shakespeare often uses it to suggest status – lower status characters would not use iambic pentameter, while kings and queens would speak in this rhythmic verse. Occasionally, when iambic pentameter is not used by a character of high status, it is there to emphasise a point in the script or that the actor is meant to say a word quickly or differently.

There are lines in the *Sir Thomas More* speech that break the rules. For example, when the character's emotions take over, Shakespeare shows him losing control of the 10-syllable structure:

To / find / a / na/tion / of / such / bar/bar/ous / tem/per

Language focus

Imagery

Throughout the speech, animal imagery is used repeatedly. When a writer uses similar imagery throughout a piece, we must ask ourselves as readers what their intentions are. Shakespeare uses animal imagery in many of his plays so we can deduce it has a dramatic purpose. It also creates a vivid image in the audience's mind, which was especially important in Elizabethan times, when there were no special effects.

In this case, animals are compared to how refugees are being treated. Shakespeare is making it clear they are dehumanised by the violence and mistreatment they are facing.

Writing questions on *Sir Thomas More*

1. How is 'like ravenous fishes' (line 15) an effective description? (2)
2. From line 16, the speech changes. Explain how and why. (2)
3. What is the effect of the rhetorical questions that run through the speech? (4)

Magid Magid is a Somali–British activist. Also known as Magid Mah and Magic Magid, he became Lord Mayor of Sheffield from May 2018 to 2019, after which he was elected to the European Parliament as Green Party MEP for Yorkshire and the Humber. He came to Britain in 1994 as a child refugee, fleeing the Somalian Civil War.

'5 Minutes with Magic Magid'

We found out how life is treating the former Mayor of Sheffield, Magid Magid.

Tell us a little bit about your background?

I was born in Somalia and came to Sheffield when I was five. I never
5 knew what I wanted to pursue as a career when I was young, but I knew I wanted to have a positive impact on those around me. I ended up taking a year out after school and worked in factories in Sheffield, before going to the University of Hull to study aquatic zoology. After that I set up a digital marketing business with two friends, it failed after a year and a bit
10 and I ended up working for the charity Shelter.

How did you get involved in politics?

The rise of UKIP in 2014 made me want to get involved with politics. I was tired of complaining and started to think about what I could do in my own community. I thought, if I could at least make Sheffield, my
15 small part of the world, better and have a positive impact then that's what I'd do. I joined the Green Party, as that's where a lot of my values lie, and decided to stand on the council in 2016. In 2018 the Lord Mayor opportunity presented itself and in May that year I became the first Green MEP for Yorkshire which was obviously a massive privilege.

20 **How did the role of mayor come about for you?**

Ultimately, it's the council that elects you, but it felt like a great opportunity to champion all that's great and good about Sheffield. I'd lie if I said there was no one who disagreed with what I said or what I was doing, some people didn't agree with my existence in that world, but it
25 was a privilege, so I made the most of it.

What are your plans now?

I'm actually starting a tour around Yorkshire and the Humber speaking to different organisations, and people to see what they want from the European Parliament. It's going to have to come back down the people,
30 it's the only way past the deadlock. I'm just trying to use my platform to highlight and challenge issues.

What was your favourite thing about being the Mayor of Sheffield?

I met amazing people every single day and learned a lot about them. I felt like Santa Claus, people would always be really excited to see me,
35 and that really motivated me to meet more people. I enjoyed surprising people, turning up to someone's graduation, crashing house parties at New Year's Eve, or inviting people around to watch *Love Actually* with me at Christmas. Normally you have a consort or a Lady Mayoress, but I didn't have one, so I'd ask members of the public to be my consort for
40 the day and pick them up to go for dinner, or an event. I tried to make them feel like Sheffield belonged to them as much as it belonged to me.

Favourite place to eat?

Jimmy's Kitchen on West Street, it does great authentic Turkish food.

How would you spend a day off?

45 I'd probably get my friends into the car, drive to Bakewell and get a Bakewell pudding with custard, just for novelty value, then I guess we'd probably end up in West Street Live.

What did you have for breakfast?

A coconut and chocolate cake. It wasn't a healthy one.

50 **Favourite film?**

City of Gods.

What is something you couldn't live without?

If I can't say my family and friends, then pizza. And ice cream.

(Source: *Living North*, September 2019)

Questions

1 What did Magid Magid study at university? (1)
2 What are your first impressions of Magid Magid? (4)
3 What is the definition of 'deadlock' (line 30)? (1)
4 In your own words, explain what 'consort' means (line 38). (1)
5 What is the effect of the organisation of the text? (4)

Text features

A soft feature

'5 Minutes with…' is what is known in journalism as a **soft feature**. Its format can be used again and again with different people and its conversational, light tone is easy to read. Can you spot any soft features in newspapers or magazines?

In '5 Minutes with…' the questions are used like subheadings with the answers as the main text below. The article is mainly Magid's voice, rather than giving a journalist's point of view about their interviewee.

Do you notice anything about the order of questions? They are chronological, which makes the 'story' easy to follow for the reader. There are short, snappy and fun questions at the end to wrap up and give some insight into the person being interviewed.

Language focus

Words can act as signposts in writing. In Magid's interview he uses **time connectives**, such as 'after that', and adverbs, such as 'ultimately', to guide a reader though his life story. However, the **register** of the article remains informal.

For example, 'then I guess we'd probably end up in West Street Live' sounds conversational and relaxed. If it were changed to 'I presume we would then visit West Street Live', it would sound more formal, as if he was talking to a stranger or writing a serious article.

Choose and then alter two other sentences from the article to put them in a formal register.

Drama focus

Monologues are speeches performed by one person. They often reveal the speaker's inner thoughts and feelings to the audience but are not heard by other characters. They include the following:

- first person pronouns: *I / me / my / mine*
- rhetorical questions: *Can you imagine it?*
- direct address to the audience: *What would you do in my situation?*

Write a monologue for a character who is halfway to safety from a war-torn country. What do they hope for? How might they be feeling?

Need an example? Check out the extract from *My Boy Jack* on page 147 of the Conflict chapter.

Perform your monologue to the class.

Writing task

You are going to write a short narrative in the **first person** about starting a new school, but this school is in an entirely different country. You will be writing as a refugee child starting at your current school.

It would be difficult to describe how different this school would be, let alone in a different language, so using the devices below will help you.

- **Figurative language**
  Comparing one thing to another will help put into words how different things are. For example: *The chairs and tables were laid out neatly like trees on the avenues back home.*
- **Sensory description**
  In a new environment, our senses are usually buzzing. So using sensory description in your story is a must. For example: *In the eating room, that they call a canteen, the aroma of sweet fruits mixed with boiled fresh vegetables was in the air.*
- **Thoughts and feelings**
  The new kid might be excited, intimidated, hopeful – probably all three things at once. Show rather than tell their feelings through your writing. For example: *My brain whirred and clanked through the maths puzzles like an old engine starting up. But I got it, I got it in the end.*

You can use the writing frame below to prepare your story:

Paragraph 1: Walking through the school gates

Thoughts and feelings. Observation of others around you. Who shows you where to go?

Paragraph 2: The first lesson

Subject or topic. How do the other children and teachers react to you? What is confusing, what is easy and what helps?

Paragraph 3: Lunchtime

What new smells, tastes and sounds do you come across? Playing with others or not. Observation of others around you.

Paragraph 4: Walking out of the gates

Thoughts and feelings about the day and about the next day.

Time to write

Now write a short narrative in first person about starting a new school. You will be the 'new kid', a refugee child, starting at your school.

Putting pen to paper

Now try one of the writing tasks below. You may want to do some of your own research before starting your piece.

1   Write a narrative about crossing dangerous terrain to get to safety.
2   Write a short story about a refugee starting a job in a new country.
3   Write a narrative based on the title, 'My new home'.

Spelling tip: irregular plural nouns

Irregular **plural nouns** are rule-breakers. They don't add 's' or 'es' as most nouns do; they completely change or don't change at all! Here are some to watch out for:

Singular	Plural
Child	Children
Man	Men
Goose	Geese
Mouse	Mice
Deer	Deer

Singular	Plural
Sheep	Sheep
Shelf	Shelves
Loaf	Loaves
Index	Indices
Curriculum	Curricula

Peer review (editing/drafting)
Reviewing your writing

Swap your writing with a partner. Read each other's work carefully, looking at:

- figurative language or sensory description – is it used effectively, or could it be improved?
- the way ideas/points of view are expressed – are they clear?
- how the narrative is structured – do the ideas link well?

Find two positive things that would improve the writing in your view. Share these with your partner.

Edit your work, considering these changes and correcting any spelling or punctuation errors.

Wider reading

If you want to read more on this topic, have a look at these brilliant books:

- *Welcome to Nowhere* by Elizabeth Laird
- *In the Sea There are Crocodiles* by Fabio Geda*
- *Boy, Everywhere* by A M Dassu
- *Shadow* by Michael Morpurgo
- *Salt to the Sea* by Ruta Sepetys
- *The Road of Bones* by Anne Fine*
- *Running on the Roof of the World* by Jess Butterworth

*Choose these titles for a more challenging read!

Book review

Prepare interview questions for an author of a book you have read recently. It might be one from the wider reading list above.

Ask a partner to read the questions. Why do they make them want to read the book?

8 Different people, different perspectives

Aims

- **Reading focus**: Using empathy to infer
- **Writing focus**: Informative writing
- **Speaking and listening focus**: Proofreading
- **Language focus**: Dialect, Standard English and informal *versus* formal writing, extended metaphor, varying sentence lengths
- **Drama focus**: Character motivation, thought-tracking

Context

In this chapter, you will meet a whole host of characters: real, imagined and inspired by real people. They are all very different people with different points of view. They may be experiencing a condition that incapacitates them but continue to be determined in their attitude to be abled, just differently. There are others who are angry, frustrated or don't have a voice at all.

You will have to put yourself in their shoes to understand their point of view, because it may be a point of view you have never come across before. Lastly, you will write an informative report about your school and how its design caters for people who have additional needs.

About the author

Annabel Pitcher is a multi-award-winning British children's author. She studied at Oxford University and became an English teacher, but she always had ambitions to become a children's author and write about realistic themes that young people could relate to. She now has four books to her name, including *Silence is Goldfish* (2015).

In this extract, Tess Turner has just discovered her father, Jack, is not her biological dad. She is shocked into silence and relies on Mr Goldfish, an imaginary friend, to share her fears and anxiety. She realises the benefits of silence quickly, but without a real-life unmute button it is difficult to free herself from her feelings.

Silence is Goldfish

I go through the motions, pretending everything's okay, which is what I need to do until I can work out what I want to do. I eat the porridge Jack makes me every morning, as he checks my homework, moving a thin finger across my Maths book, not finding any errors

5 even though it only took me twenty minutes, because I am that good at trigonometry. He hands it back with a smile that normally I would return then reminds me to pack my flute for a lesson I might not attend if I decide to run away. *It's still a possibility* I tell the goldfish inside my head, even though the plan seems ridiculous in the cold light of day. I

10 picture him, impatiently darting about beneath my bed, chanting the address of the Human Fertilisation and Embryology Authority… *One hundred and three to One hundred and five Bunhill Row in…*

'Tess?'

I come around to see Jack finish the last of his porridge then lean back

15 in his chair.

'What do you think, then?'

'Yes?'

Nine times out of ten yes is the right answer. Sure enough. Jack nods, then takes our bowls to stack in the dishwasher, strictly his domain. He

20 takes great pleasure in it, putting the plates and cups in the right order, so that we can fill the dishwasher completely, twisting his head this way and that, trying to work out where everything should go.

Today it's a plastic jug that's proving tricky. Jedi races in, scampering across the kitchen floor so that he can thrust his nose in the cutlery.

25 Jack hates it, but I love it, his pink tongue licking the butter knife with no regard for the rules.

'Out of there, boy. Come on. You know the score. Yes, that's what I thought, Tessie-T. Ask her about it. There's not a lot of point learning the flute if you don't do the grades, is there? Suzie's just done one. Do

30 you fancy having a go? We don't want to hide your light under a bushel, do we? We want to give you chance to shine. Really show what you can do, you know? Stand out.'

'I thought I was supposed to be trying to fit in?' I say, surprising myself, but not as much as Jack. He dumps the jug then straightens up.

35 'Who wants to fit in? Who wants to be ordinary?' he asks, sounding genuinely shocked. It's exhausting trying to keep up with him, and it's a genuine relief I don't have to do it anymore. 'Do you want to blend into the background, Tess? Is that what you're telling me?'

I mumble the appropriate response, but it's harder than usual. There's

40 a scream of protest in my chest where there used to be silence, and my eyes are ablaze. This is new, this heat, burning into Jack's back as he shakes his head then disappears upstairs.

I get changed in my room, grabbing an old school skirt, because my
trousers are in the wash, holding it up against my legs to see if it will
45 still fit. Probably not is my guess, given that it was a squeeze six months
ago, but with a few pulls and pushes I just about manage to get myself
into the green fabric. Shoving my feet into the black Dr Martens I wear
for school, I gaze down at my bottom half… I am big and I am strong
and I am powerful – a girl of Everest proportions who won't easily be
50 conquered. I brush my hair vigorously, then give my teeth an extra
fierce scrub, looking in the bathroom mirror at my face so full of fire.

Something's coming. I don't know what or when, but it's going to be
huge.

Annabel Pitcher

Read more

Have you enjoyed seeing
things from Tess' point
of view? Try *The Curious
Incident of the Dog in
the Night-Time* by Mark
Haddon. The narrator,
Christopher, is a person
with autism who sets out
to solve a mystery. The
book was adapted for the
stage by Simon Stephens
too, so you could always
read the script.

Questions

1 In your own words, explain what Tess means by 'I go through the
motions' (line 1). (1)
2 What is the definition of 'chanting' (line 10) in the context of the extract? (1)
3 Who is Jedi? (1) **FP**
  a the goldfish
  b Tess' sibling
  c the family dog
  d a rat
4 What musical instrument does Tess play? (1)
5 Why does she wear her school skirt? (1)

Grammar focus

Standard English

Formal writing doesn't just mean 'posh', it just means Standard English. For example, instead of saying, 'We're gonna go town' you should say, 'We are going to go to town.' You should be using Standard English for all your exam writing. Here are some tips for staying formal:

- Avoid friendly, casual words and phrases, such as 'cool', 'mate', 'you know', 'then she went', 'nice'.
- Consider your sentence starters — adverbial phrases or signpost connectives are more effective than 'But', 'Because' or 'And'.
- Avoid overusing exclamation marks!!!!!

Of course, informality can be effective when creating a character if you use it within direct speech. See more on this in the Language focus on page 130.

See more on this in the Language focus on page 130.

About the author

Louisa May Alcott (1832–1888) was an American writer most famous for her novel *Little Women*. She worked to support her family from an early age, which is why she started writing. She was an activist throughout her life, fighting for women's suffrage against slavery.

Little Women (1868) is based on many of her childhood experiences. In this extract, the eldest March sisters, Meg and Jo, and their maid, Hannah, watch over their sick sibling, Beth. The character of Beth is based on Alcott's sister, Lizzie, both of whom caught scarlet fever which weakened their bodies considerably. From then on, both the fictionalised and the real sister were treated gently, carefully and differently from the rest of their family.

Little Women

A breath of fresh air seemed to blow through the house, and something better than sunshine brightened the quiet rooms; everything appeared to feel the hopeful change; Beth's bird began to chirp again, and a half-blown rose was discovered on Amy's bush in the window.

5 The fires seemed to burn with unusual cheeriness, and every time the girls met their pale faces broke into smiles as they hugged one another, whispering, encouragingly, 'Mother's coming, dear! Mother's coming!' Everyone rejoiced but Beth; she lay in that heavy stupor, alike unconscious of hope and joy, doubt and danger. It was a piteous

10 sight, — the once rosy face so changed and vacant, the once busy hands so weak and wasted, the once smiling lips quite dumb, and the once pretty, well-kept hair scattered rough and tangled on the pillow. All day she lay so, only rousing now and then to mutter, 'Water!' with lips so parched they could hardly shape the word; all day Jo and Meg hovered

15 over her, watching, waiting, hoping, and trusting in God and mother'; and all day the snow fell, the bitter wind raged, and the hours dragged slowly by. But night came at last, and every time the clock struck the sisters, still sitting on either side of the bed, looked at each other with brightening eyes, for each hour brought help nearer. The doctor had

20 been in to say that some change for better or worse would probably take place about midnight, at which time he would return.

Hannah, quite worn out, lay down on the sofa at the bed's foot, and fell fast asleep',

25 Mr Laurence marched to and fro in the parlour, feeling that he would rather face a rebel battery than Mrs March's anxious countenance as she entered, Laurie lay on the rug, pretending to rest, but staring into the

30 fire with the thoughtful look which made his black eyes beautifully soft and clear.

Context

The extract from *Little Women* is set during the **American Civil War** (1861–1865). Find out more about why the country was at war and what the outcome was.

Mother is not with sick Beth, who is suffering from scarlet fever, because she is nursing the girls' father who has been injured in the war.

The girls never forgot that night, for no sleep came to them as they kept their watch, with that dreadful sense of powerlessness which comes to us in hours like those.

35 'If God spares Beth I never will complain again,' whispered Meg earnestly.

'If God spares Beth I'll try to love and serve Him all my life,' answered Jo, with equal fervour.

'I wish I had no heart, it aches so,' sighed Meg, after a pause.

'If life is often as hard as this, I don't see how we ever shall get through 40 it,' added her sister, despondently.

Here the clock struck twelve, and both forgot themselves in watching Beth, for they fancied a change passed over her wan face. The house was still as death, and nothing but the wailing of the wind broke the deep hush. Weary Hannah slept on, and no one but the sisters saw 45 the pale shadow which seemed to fall upon the little bed. An hour went by, and nothing happened except Laurie's quiet departure for the station. Another hour, — still no one came, and anxious fears of delays in the storm, or accidents by the way, or, worst of all, a great grief at Washington, haunted the poor girls.

50 It was past two, when Jo, who stood at the window thinking how dreary the world looked in its winding sheet[1] of snow, heard a movement by the bed, and turning quickly, saw Meg kneeling before their mother's easy chair, with her face hidden. A dreadful fear passed coldly over Jo, as she thought, 'Beth is dead, and Meg is afraid to tell me.'

55 She was back at her post in an instant, and to her excited eyes a great change seemed to have taken place. The fever flush and the look of pain were gone, and the beloved little face looked so pale and peaceful in its utter repose that Jo felt no desire to weep or lament. Leaning low over 60 this dearest of her sisters, she kissed the damp forehead with her heart on her lips, and softly whispered, 'Good-by, my Beth; good-by!'

As if waked by the stir, Hannah started out of her sleep, hurried to the bed, looked at Beth, felt her hands, listened at her lips, and then, throwing her apron over her head, sat down to rock to and fro, exclaiming, under her breath, 'The fever's turned, she's sleepin' nat'ral, her skin's damp, and 65 she breathes easy. Praise be given! Oh, my goodness me!'

Louisa May Alcott

---

1 A shroud or sheet wrapped around a dead body for burial.

Questions

1 What is the meaning of 'vacant' (line 10) in the context of the passage? (1)
2 When is the doctor due back? (1)
   a midnight
   b in the morning
   c midday
   d on Monday
3 What does Meg say she will do if Beth gets well? (1)
4 What does Hannah mean by 'The fever's turned' (line 64)? (1)

Punctuation tip: apostrophes for contraction

Contraction means shrinking, and that's what you're doing when you use an apostrophe for contraction – shrinking words.

Do not ⟶ Don't
She is ⟶ She's
You are ⟶ You're

Sometimes these **apostrophes** are called **omission** too because you put the apostrophe where a letter is missing.

Research

In the last two extracts, there is plenty to investigate. In the extract from *Silence is Goldfish*, Annabel Pitcher uses first person narration to explore how Tess is dealing with her feelings, but this technique is not just reserved for fiction books. Go to your school or local library and seek out autobiographies about real people who have experienced extraordinary personal experiences in the face of adversity. Here are some examples:

- **Christy Brown** was a famous Irish artist and writer who had **cerebral palsy**. Charities like Scope and Action Cerebral Palsy with give you more information about how varied the neurological condition is and what it means to live with it. Find out why Brown's left foot was so important.

- TikTok star **Charli D'Amelio** discusses her mental health in her book, *Essentially Charli*. Find out how she maintains confidence in the face of cyberbullying.
- **Helen Keller** was the first deaf-blind person to earn a university degree in the US. Find out how many autobiographies she wrote.

The extract from *Little Women* is set during the **American Civil War** (1861–1865).

- Find out why the country was at war and what the outcome was.
- Mother is not with sick Beth, who is suffering from scarlet fever, because she is nursing the girls' father who has been injured in the war. Have you heard of famous war nurses **Mary Seacole** and **Florence Nightingale**?

Talking point

Imagine not being able to speak your mind. Imagine not being able to share your thoughts, feelings and opinions. Imagine having so much to say but no way of saying it.

In small groups, discuss how you would feel in this situation if it was happening to you or to someone you knew, but also what you could do to share all those thoughts buzzing round in your head.

Use some of the real-life stories of overcoming adversity from the research section as inspiration.

Writing questions on *Silence is Goldfish*

1 Whose perspective is the extract written from and how is it effective? (2)
2 What is your impression of Jack? (4)
3 Re-read the penultimate paragraph. What does the author's word choice reveal about how Tess Turner is feeling? (4)
4 Consider the extract as a whole. How does the structure of this extract hook a reader in? (2)

Writing questions on *Little Women*

1 The March family have a close relationship. How can you tell? (4)
2 How does the description of the weather add to the atmosphere of the extract? (4)
3 Who is Hannah to the family and how can you tell? (3)
4 How is time used to create tension in the extract? (3)

Speaking and listening focus
Read it aloud

Reading your work aloud is often the best way to spot mistakes but also to improve your work.

Choose a recent piece of work and read it aloud to a partner. As you read, pay close attention to the punctuation, just as you would if reading from a book aloud, and pause where necessary.

Adjust your piece as you read with a different coloured pen. Maybe you need an extra comma where you paused, or you need to change a word because you've thought of a more powerful one. How many edits did you make? Now read the piece again, with the edits, to the same partner.

Listen carefully as your partner reads. Is the second reading more fluent? Have the edits helped to make it exactly how you would like to read it?

You could also record yourself reading your work and then listen back.

Thematic focus

Do you understand how the characters are feeling in the last two extracts? If you do, it's because the author has created empathy through how a character's thoughts, feelings and actions are described.

In this activity, you will explore whether we are supposed to feel empathy towards any of the characters and how the author has made us feel that. Use the table below to organise your ideas:

Character	Do you feel empathy for them? (Yes/No)	Why?/Why not? (Use evidence from the text to support your ideas.)
Tess		
Jack		
Beth		
Meg		
Jo		

Extended writing questions

You will now be writing an extended answer about an extract. Write your answer in three PEEA paragraphs, using evidence from the text to support your ideas. (See page 179 in the Exam skills chapter for an explanation of the PEEA technique.)

Here are some tips for writing extended answers:

- Read the questions carefully.
- Use the three foci in your topic sentences for the three paragraphs.
- It might help you to find your evidence for each before you start writing.
- Use connectives like 'and', 'furthermore', 'however' and 'additionally' to expand your explanations.

1 How does the author create a strong character in Extract 1?
   Consider vocabulary, sentence structure and tone.

OR

2 What effect does the structure of Extract 2 create?
   Consider sentence length, change of tone and the balance of description and dialogue.

OR

3 Write the doctor's report on Beth's condition after his first visit to the family in the *Little Women* extract and then when he returns. Explore how she looked before he left, what her family and home was like and then how her condition has improved.

Language focus
Punctuating dialogue

A great way for a writer to reveal character is to show how the character speaks. A reader can't physically hear a character speaking, so when they want to show a character's tone of voice or feelings, often punctuation is the best way to achieve this. Here are some examples:

- Using **dashes** can show they are a nervous or unsure, for example:
  I – I – I sometimes get a b-b-bit nervous.
- Character's different dialects can be shown by using apostrophes to replace letters they might miss. Here's an example from the extract above: *she's sleepin' nat'ral.*
- Using **ellipses** can show they speak slowly, for example:
  We should...go to the...cinema.

Have a go yourself the next time you're writing a character and see what **idiosyncratic** speech patterns you can create. Reading it aloud will help you perfect it too.

About the author

Raymond Antrobus is a British–Jamaican poet. He won the Ted Hughes Award for Poetry in 2019. He often writes about grief but also his experiences as a person who is deaf.

In his poem, 'Dear Hearing World' (2016), he writes about his frustration that his deafness was not celebrated in school.

---

1 Look out for the extended metaphor of space in this poem.

2 Note all the words in the semantic field of sound and noise.

4 Here the tone changes, as the pronouns change to direct address to the reader, including collective pronouns.

from 'Dear Hearing World'

I have left Earth[1] in search of sounder[2] orbits,

a solar system where the space between

a star and a planet isn't empty. I have left

a white beard of noise[3] in my place and many

of you[4] won't know the difference. We are

indeed the same volume, all of us eventually fade.

I have left Earth in search of an audible God.

I do not trust the sound of yours.

You wouldn't recognise my grandmother's *Hallelujah*

if she had to sign it, you would have made her sit

on her hands and put a ruler in her mouth

as if measuring her distance from holy.[5]

Take your God back, though his songs

are beautiful, they are not loud enough.

Raymond Antrobus

3 This metaphor describes how sound can be physical and all-encompassing.

5 This part is shocking and shows the poor treatment people who are deaf have suffered from discrimination for a long time.

Context

British Sign Language (BSL) is a sign language used in the United Kingdom and is the first or preferred language of some deaf people in the UK; other countries have their own versions, just like spoken language. There are 125 000 deaf adults in the UK who use BSL, plus an estimated 20 000 children.

It is believed that BSL had its beginnings as early as the sixteenth century but as it is not a written language, the evidence for this is scant. It only became an official language in 1975 because, beforehand, deaf children would be forced to lip-read or learn finger spelling; nevertheless, BSL was learnt unofficially.

There are many resources from which you can learn BSL. Can you find how to sign the following in BSL?

- hello
- thank you
- your initials

About the author

Tony Harrison is a British poet, translator and playwright. Harrison often draws on classical and mythical stories for his work, but also modern situations and feelings.

In 'Long Distance II' (1984), the speaker describes his father's decline in health after his mother has died.

'Long Distance II'

Though my mother was already two years dead
Dad kept her slippers warming by the gas,
put hot water bottles her side of the bed
and still went to renew her transport pass.

5   You couldn't just drop in. You had to phone.
He'd put you off an hour to give him time
to clear away her things and look alone
as though his still raw love were such a crime.

He couldn't risk my blight of disbelief
10   though sure that very soon he'd hear her key
scrape in the rusted lock and end his grief.
He knew she'd just popped out to get the tea.

I believe life ends with death, and that is all.
You haven't both gone shopping; just the same,
15   in my new black leather phone book there's your name
and the disconnected number I still call.

Tony Harrison

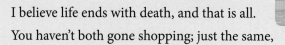

Questions

1   What is one thing that the speaker's father still does after his wife's death? (1)
2   Why couldn't the speaker 'just drop in' (line 5)? (1)
3   What is the definition of 'blight' (line 9) in the context of the poem? (1)
4   In the third stanza, where did the father hope his wife had been? (1)

Read more

Sarah Crossan is an Irish author who writes novels-in-verse. Each page is in the form of a poem but follows a clear narrative. *Toffee* is one such book that follows a runaway girl who starts to care for an older lady who has dementia.

Text features
Rhyming patterns

You will notice in 'Long Distance II' that there is a regular rhyme scheme. You can tell by looking at the end of each line:

Though my mother was already two years dead A

Dad kept her slippers warming by the gas, B

put hot water bottles her side of the bed A

and still went to renew her transport pass. B

We call this a regular ABAB rhyme scheme.

The poem also has a regular structure. There are four stanzas with four lines each.

In terms of rhythm, there are between 10 and 11 syllables per line and some enjambment, which means that the sentences are of different lengths. If you read this aloud, you'd notice it felt quite natural to read.

Your job when analysing poetry is to link these elements to the meaning of the poem.

Language focus
Extended metaphors

In the last two poems, it could be said that extended metaphors are used.

In 'Dear Hearing World', the poet uses the imagery of planets to describe how it feels to be deaf. He uses words within the same **semantic field**, such as 'orbit', 'Earth' and 'star' to achieve this extended metaphor.

In 'Long Distance II', the title as well as the 'disconnected number' at the end link to a phone call or communication, in this case to the person who has died.

Poets use extended metaphor all the time, but you can also use it in your descriptive writing. Here are some ideas:

Idea	Comparison
How it feels to be deaf	Space
Describing an avalanche	A dragon breathing fire
Unable to forget something	Having your arm in a cast

Can you write your own extended metaphor poem or a short prose description?

Writing questions on 'Long Distance II'

1 What is the effect of the rhyme and rhythm in this poem? (4)
2 In line 8, 'raw love' is used to describe the father's feelings. What is the effect of this description? (2)
3 What is your impression of the speaker? (4)
4 Why do you think the poet gave this poem its title? (3)

About the author

Sinéad Burke is an Irish writer, activist and broadcaster. At 16 years old, she began a crusade to have the fashion industry recognise people like her with **achondroplasia** and other diverse body shapes. Her various speeches and articles have now been collated for young readers in her first book.

Break the Mould: How to Take Your Place in the World

For a second, imagine what the world would look like if it was designed for me.

Think of your house, how might it look different? What about the playground? Or a
5 shop? Or a bike? Or an aeroplane? Or a car?

If the world was designed for me, if everything was built for little people, it's likely that everyone else would be disabled.

Well, maybe not everyone. I guess because you
10 and me are close to the same height, by design, my world would include you too. It would be our world.

But as you get older and taller, your back would begin to ache as you would need to bend down
15 to climb through small door frames or fill the dishwasher, or wash your hands in smaller sinks.

Trying to wash my hands and use the toilet in a public bathroom is when I remember that the world was not designed for me. I enter the
20 bathroom, queue for a cubicle, go inside...and already there's a problem.

The lock is too high for me to reach up and close it. I can't climb onto the toilet and reach over to close it either. It's too far, I'd fall.

25 I have a routine that I've practised in bathrooms all over the world. Firstly, I look for a bin. I turn it upside down, stand on it and hope that it can bear my weight. Secondly, if there is no suitable bin, I hope that reaching high and using my
30 phone to thwack the lock closed will work. Thirdly, if I still can't reach the lock, I take off my jacket and bag and lay them on the ground of the cubicle just at the divide between the door and the wall, hoping that someone outside
35 will notice that I'm inside and won't try to come in. But, if there is no suitable bin, if my phone won't work and if I'm not wearing a coat or a bag...I ask a stranger for help.

I open the door and scan the people to see who
40 looks the kindest, though it's difficult to tell. I'll pick someone and say, 'Hi, I'm Sinéad. I am sorry to bother you, but I can't reach the lock to close the door and I really need to use the bathroom, would you mind standing outside
45 the door, to make sure no one comes in, please?'

'Sure, no problem.'

It's what they always say. My independence is rooted in strangers' kindness.

I use the toilet and leave the cubicle. I need to
50 wash my hands.

But the sink, soap dispenser and hand dryer are all out of reach. I imagine that you have experienced this too, given that most bathrooms are built for average-height adults. I've learned
55 to carry hand sanitiser with me to ensure that my hands are clean, even when I can't reach the sink.

Often, I'll visit the disabled or accessible bathroom just to wash my hands because there,
60 the sink, soap dispenser and hand-dryer are all lower, as is the lock on the door. But, the toilet is too high for me. It is designed at that height so that wheelchair users can transfer from their chair to the toilet with ease. It makes sense and

65 is necessary, but it shows that even when we design for disabled people, we sometimes still only design for one kind of disability.

But it isn't just disabled people who might feel like the world isn't designed for them. There
70 are times that you could have felt this way too. Have you ever noticed the colour of plasters that we use to cover up small cuts and grazes? The people who design these plasters say that the colour is nude, by which they mean it's the
75 colour of skin. But, whose skin? The colour of people's skin can vary so much and these 'nude' plasters are really only nude for one particular skin colour. Whether it's public bathrooms, clothing, plasters, ballet slippers, or the design
80 of buildings, the way the world is built can either make life easy or much harder for some people.

Sinéad Burke

Text features
Anecdotes

Anecdotes are key to Burke's writing. They illustrate her points, sometimes in excruciating detail (for example, 'I have a routine that I've practised in bathrooms all over the world'), so the reader can understand the point she's making. She wants us to know how difficult using a public bathroom is, so she goes step by step and asks rhetorical questions such as 'But, whose skin?' along the way so we can empathise with her, rather than just sympathise.

In some instances, anecdotes can be used for humour and Burke brings in some witty lines to soften the message. For example, 'I hope that reaching high and using my phone to thwack the lock closed will work'. The word choice of 'thwack' makes us laugh and warm to her, and in turn warm to what she's saying. Even though we may not be in her shoes, she is relatable and we understand her point of view.

By using anecdotes and humour, Burke achieves our empathy and understanding.

Questions

1 In lines 47–48, Burke says 'My independence is rooted in strangers' kindness.' Comment on why this is an effective description. (2)
2 In what ways does Burke's writing style engage a reader? (4)
3 What is your impression of Sinéad Burke? (4)
4 Summarise Sinéad Burke's main message in this extract. (2)

Language focus
Varying sentence lengths

Burke is almost as famous for her writing as she is her public speaking, so we can learn a lot from how she writes to engage an audience. One of these ways is by using a variety of sentence lengths. It is an important device to keep the audience engaged, whether they are reading or listening, and Burke does just that by including short sentences, multi-clausal sentences and interrogative sentences (questions). This variety keeps us 'on our toes' and ensures she is able to pause and breathe if she is speaking to an audience.

Can you spot the different sentence types in the text?

Need a reminder about sentence types? Head to Growing up for more on simple sentences (page 12), Journeying for compound sentences (page 60) and Inventive inventions for complex sentences (page 94).

Drama focus

As a class, split into four groups. One group will sit on the ground and cannot move. The second group should cover their ears, possibly with headphones. The third group is not allowed to speak and, finally, the fourth group should cover their eyes.

Imagine it is breaktime at school. Consider how your limitation would affect you during this time.

Your teacher will then walk around and hold their hand over your head. When they do, it is your turn to speak. Explain how you feel about not being able to walk, hear, speak or see. Listen to each other.

Writing task

You are going to write an informative report about how the design of your school is accessible and inclusive. You could include the playground, the toilets or the canteen and getting around the building.

This is a straightforward type of writing in which you must inform your audience clearly and in detail. Even though you are describing different places, figurative language can be used, but the majority of the language should be literal. Use signpost connectives to guide a reader and keep your sentences interesting and varied.

Use the plan below to help you write this report but remember, the places listed in the question are only suggestions so you can choose your own.

Introduction

Explain what your report is about and what it covers.

Paragraph 1: The playground

Describe the playground and its facilities. Weigh up the good aspects and bad aspects which make it inaccessible.

Paragraph 2: The toilets

Describe the toilets and where they are in the building. If there is a disabled option, where is it? Consider their design – how wide are they? How high are the sinks? How much light is there?

Paragraph 3: Getting around the building

Describe the average day of travel around the school. Is there a lift? How wide are the corridors? Are rooms easy to find? How many pupils move around at one time?

Conclusion

Sum up your findings. It is here that you can give your opinion and key recommendations.

Time to write

Write an informative report about how the design of your school is accessible and inclusive. You could include: the playground, the toilets or the canteen and getting around the building.

Putting pen to paper

Now try one of the writing tasks below. You may want to do some of your own research before starting your piece.

1   Write a blog post about a visit to a museum or art gallery, describing how they have made their building accessible and inclusive.
2   Write the text for an information pamphlet about how retail stores can be made more welcoming to people with disabilities.
3   Write a news report on the achievements of a Paralympian.

Spelling tip: all together *versus* altogether

Is it 'all together' or 'altogether'?

'All together' means 'in a group', for example: *Let's go all together to the party*.

'Altogether' means 'completely', for example: *It was altogether a terrible party*.

Peer review (editing/drafting)

Reviewing your writing

Swap your writing with a partner. Read each other's work carefully, looking at:

- the way ideas/points of view are expressed – are they clear
- how the essay/article is structured – do the ideas link well?

Find two positive things that would improve the writing in your view. Share these with your partner.

Edit your work, considering these changes and correcting any spelling or punctuation errors.

Wider reading

If you want to read more about the experiences of people with different abilities, try these brilliant books:

- *Goldfish Boy* by Lisa Thompson
- *Face Like Glass* by Frances Hardinge*
- *The Harder They Fall* by Bali Rai
- *We Are All Made of Molecules* by Susin Nielsen

*Choose this title for a more challenging read!

Book review

Write a letter to the author of a book you have read recently. It might be one from the wider reading list above.

Ask a partner to read the letter. What do they think of the book from what you have written? Does it make them want to read the book?

9 Conflict

Aims

- **Reading focus**: Analysing language, how writers imply meaning
- **Writing focus**: Description
- **Speaking and listening focus**: Active listening
- **Language focus**: Monologue, diary, relative pronouns, sentence starters
- **Drama focus**: Creating characters through direction

Context

Conflict comes in all shapes and sizes. You can have a conflict of interest, an internal conflict or a physical fight, but we will be looking at the theme of war. War is a complex issue, as you have probably learnt in History lessons, but perhaps its greatest complexity is its impact on people. In all the political and military negotiation, it is often the civilians that are forgotten.

You will encounter war in many variations in this chapter. We start with an alien invasion, then read as young men go 'over the top' in the First World War and we meet a young girl living amidst a civil war. All conflicts have consequences though, so we will be considering them in an extract about a family's reaction to a missing son, and another extract when a wider conflict in society makes it into school life. Finally, you will be writing a detailed description about a conflict zone, real or imagined.

About the author

H G Wells (1866–1946) is often referred to as the 'father of science-fiction' because of his forward-thinking and imaginative writing. He foresaw many of the technological advances of the late-twentieth century and is thus known as a futurist. His work has also inspired scientists to innovate and develop their own ideas based on his.

The War of the Worlds (1898) is about an invasion of Earth by Martians. In 1938 it was dramatised on the radio in America and caused widespread panic because it was so realistic that some people thought it was really happening. In the following extract, the Martians have landed in Surrey and their craft is sitting in a huge crater caused by their landing.

The War of the Worlds

Suddenly there was a flash of light, and a quantity of luminous greenish smoke came out of the pit in three distinct puffs, which drove up, one after the other, straight into the still air.

This smoke (or flame, perhaps, would be the better word for it) was so
5 bright that the deep blue sky overhead and the hazy stretches of brown common towards Chertsey, set with black pine-trees, seemed to darken abruptly as these puffs arose, and to remain the darker after their dispersal. At the same time a faint hissing sound became audible.

Beyond the pit stood the little wedge of people with the white flag at its
10 apex, arrested by these phenomena, a little knot of small vertical black shapes upon the black ground. As the green smoke rose, their faces flashed in pallid green, and faded again as it vanished. Then slowly the hissing passed into a humming, into a long, loud, droning noise. Slowly a humped shape rose out of the pit, and the ghost of a beam of light
15 seemed to flicker out from it.

Forthwith flashes of actual flame, a bright glare leaping from one to another, sprang from the scattered group of men. It was as if some invisible jet impinged upon them and flashed into white flame. It was as if each man were suddenly and momentarily turned to fire.

20 Then, by the light of their own destruction, I saw them staggering and falling, and their supporters turning to run.

I stood staring, not as yet realising that this was death leaping from man to man in that little distant crowd. All I felt was that it was something very strange. An almost noiseless and blinding flash of
25 light, and a man fell headlong and lay still; and as the unseen shaft of heat passed over them, pine-trees burst into fire, and every dry furze-bush became with one dull thud a mass of flames. And far away towards Knaphill I saw the flashes of trees and hedges and wooden buildings suddenly set alight.

30 It was sweeping round swiftly and steadily, this flaming death, this invisible, inevitable sword of heat. I perceived it coming towards me by the flashing bushes it touched, and was too astounded and stupefied to stir. I heard the crackle of fire in the sand-pits and the sudden squeal of a horse that was as suddenly stilled. Then it was as if
35 an invisible yet intensely heated finger were drawn through the heather between me and the Martians, and all along a curving line beyond the sand-pits the dark ground smoked and crackled. Something fell with a crash far away to the left of the common. Forthwith the hissing and humming ceased, and the black, dome-like object sank slowly out of
40 sight into the pit.

All this happened with such a swiftness that I had stood motionless, dumbfounded and dazzled by the flashes of light. Had that death swept through a full circle, it must inevitably have slain me in my surprise. But it passed and spared me, and left the night about me
45 suddenly dark and unfamiliar.

The undulating common seemed now dark almost to blackness, except where its roadways lay grey and pale under the deep-blue sky of the early night. It was dark, and suddenly void of men. Overhead the stars were mustering, and in the west the sky was still a pale, bright, almost
50 greenish blue.

HG Wells

Questions

1 What colour is the smoke? (1)
2 What is the definition of 'dispersal' (line 8)? (1)
3 What language technique is used in 'long, loud, droning noise' (line 13)? (1)
4 What are the two place names that the narrator mentions? (2)
5 Find a quote that shows that the narrator survives the attack. (1)

Read more

Looking for some non-fiction about conflict? *The Diary of a Young Girl* by Anne Frank is a great starting point. 13-year-old Anne and her Jewish family are forced to hide above her father's office in Amsterdam when the Nazi agenda against the Jewish community comes into full force. Her diary is full of any normal teenager's concerns, but the looming danger is never far away.

Grammar focus
Relative clauses

Relative clauses are a type of **subordinate clause**. They modify and give more information about a noun. They are introduced by **relative pronouns**:

that who whose which that when where

Here is an example of how they are constructed:

The narrator stared at the spaceships[1], which[2] had arrived that morning[3].

3 relative clause	**1** noun to be modified	**2** relative pronoun

Use 'who' or 'whose' when discussing a person.

Use 'when' or 'where' when you are explaining the time or place.

One way to check whether you should use a 'that' or a 'which' is whether it is a singular or a plural noun. For example:

*The window, **that** had been cleaned, was sparkling.*

*The windows, **which** had been cleaned, were sparkling.*

Try using all the different relative pronouns in sentences of your own.

About the author

Sally Gardner is a British author and illustrator. She began her career as a theatrical set designer and then went on to be a writer. She now writes and illustrates for a wide range of readers. *Maggot Moon* has also been adapted for the stage by the Unicorn Theatre.

Maggot Moon (2013) is a dystopian novel where a ruthless regime, the Motherland, has taken hold. Standish, the narrator, tells us that suspicions and mistrust are rife. Standish's friend, Hector, has been abducted, and now the leather-coat man is definitely watching him, but he still has to go to school. The conflicts within society are just as stark there. Hans (a member of the Motherland Youth) spies on other children and bullies them mercilessly.

Maggot Moon

Hans Fielder was his old self now there was no more Hector to cramp his style. He was the drawing pin. He sent his merry men to round me up and push me behind the bench.

'What would an officer want with a dunce?'

5 'You mean the leather-coat man?' I said. I saw that Hans Fielder was wound up tighter than a clockwork soldier, ready to do battle.

'Of course I mean him, you fricking moron.'

You see, Hans Fielder had from birth greedily drunk all this Motherland sheep milk. Mrs Fielder has eight, nine, ten, eleven

10 children. Can't remember, not good at counting sheep. What I know is that she and her husband survive on their rewards for the patriotic support of the Motherland. They take pride in their work, which is to report on all the good citizens who don't toe the party line. Yes, these Fielders have well-fed, well-clothed children.

15 It's easy to spot the parents who are collaborators in our school. Their sons wear long trousers. I, like most of the underclass, wear shorts that once were trousers before I grew too long for them. Now they are cut off below the knee, the two drain pipes of fabric kept in my mother's sewing box in case repairs are necessary.

20 Hans Fielder, of the long trousers and the new school blazer, pushed me up hard against the playground wall and asked the question again. His sidekicks all gathered round.

I didn't fight back when they started in on me again.

Gramps once said, 'Whatever else you do, Standish, don't raise your
25 fists. Turn away. If they throw you out of that school, well…'

He never finished what he was saying. There was no need.

But I couldn't keep quiet any longer.

Hans Fielder stopped punching me.

'What about my mother?' he asked.

30 'How she informs on people, makes up lies, sends innocent people to the maggot farms – to keep you in new trousers.'

That stopped him. Doubt is a great worm in a crispy, red apple. You didn't need to be a rocket scientist to know who the real idiots were here: Hans Fielder who believed he was destined for greatness,
35 along with his merry gang. They were all bleating sheep, the whole maladjusted lot of them. They never questioned anything. There was not one of a rare breed of Whys among them, just plain, shorn, bleached sheep. The brain-branded idiots couldn't see that, like all the rest of us who lived in Zone Seven, they were never going anywhere.

40 The only chance Hans Fielder had of escape was to be sent to fight the Obstructors, and that was as good as booking yourself a slot in the crematorium. But that realisation had yet to dawn on him.

So the beating continued. I thought of my flesh as a wall. The me inside the wall they can't bully, they can't touch, so while they beat the drum
45 of my skin I thought hard about that leather-coat man and where his black Jag was going next. In my mind's eye I could see it arriving in our road. He wasn't going to have any problems finding where we live. After all, it was the only row of houses left standing. I saw the leather-coat man finding our hens, the TV, pushing Gramps down to the cellar,
50 and, worst of all, discovering the moon man. I was seeing this all in my head like a film being played and ending badly.

'Standish Treadwell,' shouted Mr Gunnell, 'what are you doing behind there? The bell has gone.'

I hadn't even noticed it. I tasted the blood in my mouth, felt my nose
55 and thought, at least it isn't broken.

Sally Gardner

Questions

1 What language technique is used in 'He was the drawing pin' (line 2)? (1)
2 What does the narrator compare collaborators to in lines 8–9? (1)
3 What zone number do Standish and Hans live in? (1)
4 Who is Mr Gunnell? (1)
   a a teacher
   b a police officer
   c a bus driver
   d a football coach **FP**

Punctuation tip: hyphens and dashes

A hyphen is different to a dash.

A hyphen is shorter in length and used to join words or prefixes. For example:

twenty-two   co-operation   empty-handed

A dash is longer and used to join clauses in a sentence. For example:

The astronaut – an excellent engineer – fixed the spacecraft.

Research

Choose a mid- to late-twentieth-century war you'd like to know more about and research the following. It might be an international war, a civil war or a war between regions. At this stage, look for facts rather than feelings.

- Who was fighting whom?
- What was the catalyst for the war?
- Where was the main conflict zone?
- What were the major events of this war?
- Were there protests against the war and what were their arguments?
- What was the outcome?

Talking point: the victims of war

In small groups, share your findings about the wars you researched above. Once you have shared the facts, use your inference and deduction skills to discuss who the victims of the war were. What did they have to face and what were the consequences of the conflict on their lives? Put yourselves in their shoes as you discuss.

Writing questions on *The War of the Worlds*

1   What is ironic about the 'white flag' in line 9? (3)
2   Read lines 30–40. How does the author create a vivid description of the narrator's near-fatal encounter? (6)
3   In your opinion, why do you think the narrator does not run away? (2)
4   Find two examples of how sound is used in this extract and comment on its effect. (4)

Writing questions on *Maggot Moon*

1   Read lines 10–14. In your own words, explain why some people choose to collaborate with the Motherland. (3)
2   Read lines 35–38. How does the author use imagery in these lines to form a vivid description of collaborators? Refer to the text closely in your answer. (4)
3   What is your impression of Standish from this extract? (4)
4   In your opinion, why does Standish not fight back? (3)

Speaking and listening focus
Active listening

Listen to a partner's answers to the last comprehension questions. Give them your undivided attention. It's hard, isn't it? Listening is a key skill though and very useful for life, not just school. We need to practise actively listening to do it well. The Chinese character for the word 'listening' splits up the skill into five parts, which you can follow when practising:

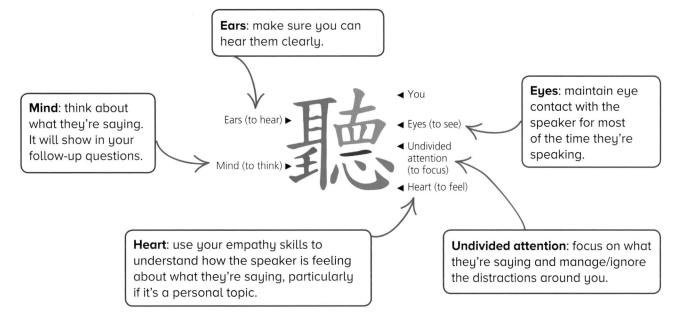

Ears: make sure you can hear them clearly.

Eyes: maintain eye contact with the speaker for most of the time they're speaking.

Mind: think about what they're saying. It will show in your follow-up questions.

You
Eyes (to see)
Ears (to hear) ▶
Undivided attention (to focus)
Mind (to think) ▶
Heart (to feel)

Heart: use your empathy skills to understand how the speaker is feeling about what they're saying, particularly if it's a personal topic.

Undivided attention: focus on what they're saying and manage/ignore the distractions around you.

Thematic focus

Both extracts are written in the first person, but narrators react differently to the conflicts they face. While Standish seems fully versed on the Motherland's rules, the narrator in *The War of the Worlds* is 'dumbfounded' by the invaders. On the other hand, in the face of adversity, neither run away. Complete the table below, adding any reactions that you note in the extracts:

	Reaction 1	Possible explanation	Reaction 2	Possible explanation
Narrator Extract 1	Fascinated	Never seen anything like this before, Victorian times so lack of technology	Dumbfounded	
Narrator Extract 2	*But I couldn't keep quiet any longer.*	Frustration, last straw, can't mentally hurt him		

Extended writing questions

You will now be writing an extended answer about an extract. Write your answer in three PEEA paragraphs, using evidence from the text to support your ideas. (See page 179 in the Exam skills chapter for an explanation of the PEEA technique.)

Here are some tips for writing extended answers:

- Read the questions carefully.
- Use the three foci in your topic sentences for the three paragraphs.
- It might help you to find your evidence for each before you start writing.
- Use connectives like 'and', 'furthermore', 'however' and 'additionally' to expand your explanations.

1 How does the author create a sense of the unknown in Extract 1 from *The War of the Worlds*?

   Comment on the use of language, vocabulary and narrative perspective in your answer.

OR

2 How does the author create tension in Extract 2 from *Maggot Moon*?

   Consider the use of imagery, structure and narrative perspective in your answer.

OR

3 As one of the aliens from *The War of the Worlds*, write a report back to your home planet about the attack. You should explore what the smoke signified, the purpose of destroying the group of humans and what the aliens' next step would be.

Language focus
Multiple adjectives

Both Wells and Gardner use multiple adjectives to add detail to their descriptions. Here are some examples:

just plain, shorn, bleached sheep

the sky was still a pale, bright, almost greenish blue.

By adding more detail to your descriptions, you're bringing the scene to life for a reader. Gardener could have just described the colour of the sheep, but she tells us about the texture too, which suggests their conformity and perhaps thuggishness. Wells could have just said the sky was 'pale' but the contrast of 'bright' and then the weirdness of 'greenish' makes us think that this is not normal.

Try adding extra adjectives to see for yourself what impact it has on your own writing.

About the author

David Haig is an English actor and playwright. He has been a stage and screen actor for four decades and has won an Olivier Award.
My Boy Jack (1997) was his first play and it premiered at Hampstead Theatre. The play is set during the First World War.

About the author

This monologue ends Act One, just as the young men are about to go 'over the top'. John (or Jack) is based on the real-life son of Rudyard Kipling who died in battle in 1915 aged 18.

1 The impact of silence on stage is just as important as sound; it builds tension and atmosphere.

2 Here, lighting helps signify that we are listening to John's thoughts and he's not saying his lines to the other characters.

3 Playwrights can use italics in their scripts to suggest how an actor says the line.

4 These dashes clearly show pauses, perhaps John's nervous state too, but a director could use them as moments for the actors to move, which would add to the overall look of the scene.

5 Using this term of endearment shows how young he is and is not something he'd say out loud in front of his peers. It is also a jolt to the audience as it is unexpected.

6 This means all lights out. Blackout is often used to end scenes but is also very dramatic.

My Boy Jack

BOWE scrambles in the mud, but then gives up. He stands, strained, motionless. The seconds pass. Someone coughs. The sound of equipment moving as a soldier shifts his weight from one foot to the other. Silence[1]. JOHN takes off his glasses for a final time, and as he dries them, the lights close in on his face and we penetrate his thoughts[2].

JOHN   I'm *so* frightened.[3]

My heart is beating everywhere, behind my eyes, down my legs, in my chest…pulsing, hammering.

It's cold.

Please God, I mustn't let them down. Will I be brave? Will I fail? –[4] Onto the firestep – keep the pistol out of the mud – left hand on the parapet – pull – right foot on the sand bags – push up – left leg over – Straighten – run – I mustn't let them down. Some of these men will be dead tonight. I may be dead tonight. Let me live. Stop raining – just for a second.

Oh Daddo[5] – what a luxury – to turn on a hot water tap – hot steaming water – evening clothes – dinner at the Ritz – the Alhambra afterwards. Elsie. Mother. Daddo. – My first action – Fifteen seconds – is that the whistle? – one clear blast – left hand – parapet – sand bags – over – run. Run fast and straight. Please God let me live. Pistol high – run, run, run.

The silence is broken by twenty, thirty whistles sounding all down the line. JOHN looks at his watch. Zero Hour. He blows his whistle. BOWE, DOYLE, MCHUGH and JOHN climb up and over. MCHUGH and DOYLE let out a long, primal, piercing scream to defy their fear. The sound cuts through the noise of the attack.

Blackout.[6]

End of Act One.

David Haig

My Boy Jack by David Haig is based on Rudyard Kipling's grief surrounding his son's death in the First World War. Kipling (1865–1936) was a famous writer, who was the first Briton to win the Nobel Prize for Literature, and is probably best known for *The Jungle Book*, but he was also a poet. The play's title comes from Kipling's poem entitled 'My Boy Jack'.

John (or Jack) was originally declined by the army because of his poor eyesight but his father managed to persuade some military contacts otherwise.

In this extract, John's parents have just heard that he is missing in action. They must share the news with their other child, Elsie, who is preparing for a birthday party they are due to attend.

My Boy Jack is set during the First World War. Find out more about the 'Great War' by researching these questions to get you started:
- Where did the main fighting take place?
- What does 'trench warfare' mean?
- What new technology was used in the battles?
- What was the role of women during the war?
- How did the war end?
- Why have poppies become a symbol of the First World War?

My Boy Jack

	CARRIE	You should have stopped him.
	RUDYARD	All of Jack's friends, to a man, every one of them, is in France. Do you think for one moment that I could have dissuaded him?
5	CARRIE	The point is, that you never tried.
	RUDYARD	No I didn't.
	CARRIE	Nor did you want to stop him.
	RUDYARD	No… Why should I? Why should I stop him? If I had, he would have suffered a living death here, ashamed and despised by everyone. Could you bear that? […] It's true. How would he hold his head up, whilst his friends risked death in France? How would he walk down the high street, or into a shop? He wouldn't. He would stay indoors, growing weaker and quieter by the day. Unable to leave his room. And he would wish he was dead.
10		
15		
	CARRIE	People would understand.
	RUDYARD	No they would not. They know what we are fighting for. They know we must go forward, willing to sacrifice everything to deliver mankind from evil.
20	CARRIE	Yes that's very fine. But will you believe that tomorrow? Today is the last day you can believe that.
	RUDYARD	Carrie, if by any chance Jack is dead, it will have been the finest moment in his young life. We would not wish him to outlive that.
25	CARRIE	You don't believe that Rud. I know you don't. There is no need to say that to me.

Long pause. RUDYARD says nothing. Then the door is flung open and ELSIE is there. She is carrying four unwrapped birthday presents, plus brown paper, string, labels, scissors, etc. She dumps it all on the table.

30	ELSIE	Hello!
	RUDYARD	Hello Bird.

	ELSIE	What are you drinking?
	RUDYARD	Whisky.
	ELSIE	But it's only a quarter to twelve.
35	RUDYARD	Well never mind. It tastes jolly good.

ELSIE holds up a paper bag with something in it.

	ELSIE	This is from Jack. I think he'd approve.

She looks at CARRIE, then RUDYARD. Silence.

He's been killed.

40	RUDYARD	No…no he's missing.
	ELSIE	Missing?
	RUDYARD	Believed wounded.

ELSIE says nothing. Silence. She looks at her parents. She then picks up a piece of wrapping paper and folds it in two, creasing it sharply. She cuts down the crease and places a present on one of the halves of paper. She carefully wraps it. RUDYARD and CARRIE watch her.

	RUDYARD	Bird…
	ELSIE	He'll come home then…he'll be fine. How are we doing for time?
50	CARRIE	Not well.
	ELSIE	Mother?

She hands a present and a sheet of paper to CARRIE. ELSIE picks up some string and neatly ties up her parcel.

Mother?

CARRIE starts to wrap her parcel. RUDYARD picks up a piece of paper.

	RUDYARD	Do we need to go?
	ELSIE	Very rude if we don't. At this notice.

RUDYARD wraps his parcel. No-one says anything. The sounds of paper, scissors, wooden boxes on a table. ELSIE cuts lengths of string and then writes her label. She passes pen and label to CARRIE. CARRIE writes her label. ELSIE takes JOHN's present out of the bag. Suddenly she is still. She looks at RUDYARD.

Why did you let him go?

RUDYARD struggles to control his anger.

65	RUDYARD	No sacrifice…is too great…no sacrifice, however painful, is too great…if we win the day…
	ELSIE	*(angry and upset)* You've missed the point haven't you? God! You just… You've no idea. God!

Silence. RUDYARD and CARRIE are helpless.

David Haig

Questions

1 What is the first name of Jack's mother? (1)
2 What is Elsie's nickname? (1)
3 What time of day is it? (1)
4 Elsie is excited and happy by the news about her brother. True or false? (1) **FP**
5 What is the definition of 'sacrifice' (line 65)? (1)

Writing questions on *My Boy Jack*

1 In your own words, explain why Rudyard did not feel that he could stop his son from going to war. (3)
2 How do the stage directions demonstrate how the tension between the family grows during the scene? (4)
3 How does Elsie react to the news? Refer to evidence from the text to support your points. (4)

Text features
Stage directions

The stage directions are important in a drama script, particularly when we analyse a drama script. They give us insight into how the playwright imagined the set to be designed, or what they wanted the actors to do, or how they wanted them to say certain lines. In this extract, the playwright is also, very clear about the props.

'Props' is short for 'theatrical property'. These are the objects handled by the actors on stage. Anything that's portable or moveable is usually referred to as a prop.

Look closely at the props noted in this extract. They signify the party, the happy event that the characters are due to attend. But then they're used to build tension between the family members as they try to keep a semblance of normality in the face of grief.

What other props might they have on stage during this scene?

Language focus
Natural-sounding dialogue

Playwrights work hard to make their writing as natural as possible because the purpose of it is to be spoken. As we naturally speak in shorter sentences than we write, that's why most of the sentences in drama scripts are short. For example:

Well never mind. It tastes jolly good.

When they are longer, they are broken up by punctuation, making it easy for an actor to break up the line with breaths and add emotion into a line. For example:

No sacrifice...is too great...no sacrifice, however painful, is too great...if we win the day...

Extended writing questions

You will now be writing an extended answer to the question below. Write your answer in three PEEA paragraphs, using evidence from the text to support your ideas. (See page 179 in the Exam skills for an explanation of the PEEA technique.)

Here are some tips for writing extended answers:

● Read the questions carefully.
● Use the three foci in your topic sentences for the three paragraphs.
● It might help you to find your evidence for each before you start writing.
● Use connectives 'and', 'furthermore', 'however' and 'additionally' to expand your explanations.

How does the playwright, David Haig, make this scene engaging and thought-provoking?

Consider these three points:

● the presentation of the relationships between the characters
● dramatic effects, including through the use of stage directions
● what the scene suggests about Kipling as a father.

About the author

Zlata Filipović was given a diary just before her tenth birthday in 1991 and began to write in it regularly, naming it Mimmy or Mimme. Growing up in Sarajevo reads much the same as it would anywhere else, but the mood changes as war gets ever closer. Zlata and her family remain in the city while her friends' families escape and Zlata's world starts to fall apart.

Her diary was published in 1992 by UNICEF to raise awareness. The family stayed in the city until 1993 when they escaped to Paris with help from the United Nations, finally settling in Dublin.

Zlata's Diary

Thursday, 7 May 1992

Dear Mimme,

I was almost positive the war would stop, but today... Today a shell fell on the park in front of my house, the park where I used to play with
5 my girlfriends. A lot of people were hurt. From what I hear Jaca, Jaca's mother, Selma, Nina, our neighbour Dado and who knows how many other people who happened to be there were wounded. Dado, Jaca and her mother have come home from hospital, Selma lost a kidney but I don't know how she is, because she's still in hospital. AND NINA IS DEAD.
10 A piece of shrapnel[1] lodged in her brain and she died. She was such a sweet, nice little girl. We went to kindergarten together, and we used to play together in the park. Is it possible I'll never see Nina again? Nina, an innocent eleven-year-old little girl – the victim of a stupid war. I cry and wonder why? She didn't do anything. A disgusting war has destroyed a
15 young child's life. Nina, I'll always remember you as a wonderful little girl.

Love, Mimmy,

Zlata

> **1** Fragment of a bomb or shell thrown out by an explosion.

Wednesday, 13 May 1992

Dear Mimmy,

20 Life goes on. The past is cruel, and that's exactly why we should forget it.

The present is cruel too and I can't forget it. There's no joking with war. My present reality is the cellar, fear, shells, fire.

Terrible shooting broke out the night before last. We were afraid that we might be hit by shrapnel or a bullet, so we ran over to the Bobars'.
25 We spent all of that night, the next day and the next night in the cellar and in Nedo's flat. (Nedo is a refugee from Grbavica[2]. He left his parents and came here to his sister's empty flat.) We saw terrible scenes on TV. The town in ruins, burning, people and children being killed. It's unbelievable.

30 The phones aren't working, we haven't been able to find out anything about Grandma and Grandad, Melica, how people in other parts of town are doing. On TV we saw the place where Mummy works, Vodoprivreda, all in flames. It's on the aggressor's side of town (Grbavica). Mummy cried. She's depressed. All her years of work and effort – up in flames.
35 It's really horrible. All around Vodoprivreda there were cars burning, people dying, and nobody could help them. God, why is this happening?

I'M SO MAD I WANT TO SCREAM AND BREAK EVERYTHING!

Your Zlata

Thursday, 14 May, 1992

40 Dear Mimmy,

The shelling here has stopped. Daddy managed to run over to Grandma's and Grandad's to see how they are, how they've been coping with the madness of the past few days. They're all right, thank God. Melica and her family are all right, and Grandma heard from Vinko that Meda and
45 Bojan (an aunt and her son) are also all right.

2 A residential area in the city of Sarajevo.

The situation at the Marshal Tito barracks and in the new parts of town is terrible. It's a madhouse around the electricity board building and the radio and television centre. I can't watch television any more. I can't bear to. The area around Otes seems to be the only place that is still quiet.
50 Mummy's brother Braco and his family live there. They're so lucky, there's no shooting where they live.

Zlata

Sunday, 17 May 1992

Dear Mimmy,

55 It's now definite: there's no more school. The war has interrupted our lessons, closed down the schools, sent children to cellars instead of classrooms. They'll give us the grades we got at the end of last term. So I'll get a report card saying I've finished fifth grade.

Ciao!

60 Zlata

Zlata Filipović

Questions

1 What language technique is used in 'the past is cruel' (line 20) and what effect does it have? (2)
2 Where does Zlata's mother work? (1)
3 What school grade is Zlata in? (1)
4 How can you tell that Zlata is a young girl? Refer to the text closely in your answer. (4)

Text features
Diaries

Diaries written at important moments in history become important artefacts. They capture a moment in time through an individual's eyes so can become significant to us when we are learning about social history.

Whether diaries are written to be read or just written to express unspoken feelings, they usually include the following elements:

- a date above each entry
- written in **first person**
- informal tone and style (particularly in modern diary writing)
- personal opinions
- they may include an **addressee** or sign off, just like Zlata's, but that's usually reserved for diaries of younger people.

Language focus

Informal style

Zlata's writing style in her diary is informal, which is to be expected: it is her personal recollection, she is quite young and her diary was written in modern times. One way she is informal is in the way she uses capitalisation. For example:

I'M SO MAD I WANT TO SCREAM AND BREAK EVERYTHING!

Her frustration is evident here. You have probably used capitalisation in digital communications to show strong emotions but, unless we're writing informally, we only use it in for the following reasons:

- to mark the beginning of a sentence or of direct speech
- for proper nouns (names of people, places, days, months)
- titles of books, TV shows, films, plays, poems, holidays, etc.

Drama focus

In small groups, read through the extract from *My Boy Jack*. Using just your voices, convey the different characters' emotions through tone, volume, pitch and pace.

Now get your performance 'on its feet'! How can you portray those same emotions through your body language, movement and gestures? Try out different people in different roles and then reflect on how different or similar the performances were.

Writing task

You are going to write a description of a conflict zone. The conflict can be real or imagined and in any time period you like. You may want to base your description on something you've read or researched in this chapter.

Remember, description is not the same as narrative. You are not telling a story, so you need to avoid plot points or characters. Writing in **third person** works best for description so you can keep a distance as an **omniscient narrator**. Use the ideas in the table to guide your writing:

Sentence starters

Making your sentence starters varied and descriptive will keep your reader engaged. Try out some of these sentence starters in your writing:

- **The power of three** starter, for example, '**Cold, tired and hungry**, the soldiers were sat on the dusty ground.'
- The alliterative starter, for example, '**W**aving **w**ildly from side to side, the flag was raised.'
- The 'as if' starter, for example, '**As if** searching for long-forgotten memories, she dug her hands into her pockets.'
- The simile starter, for example, '**Like a cat stalking its prey**, the plane tailed its counterpart.'

Figurative language

We use figurative language when we're describing something that's difficult to put into words. Comparing an object, event, scene or feeling to something else in a **metaphor**, **personification** or **simile** is helpful, especially with a difficult theme like conflict. You could add in extra adjectives here to add more detail too (see page 81).

Sensory description

Use your senses to bring the scene to life. What you see, hear and smell are usually the simplest senses to describe, but make sure you use precise adjectives. For example, rather than saying, 'The smell of gunpowder was in the air' say, 'The pungent, choking smell of gunpowder was in the air'.

Taste and touch can be harder to describe. But remember all our senses are connected so you may smell and taste something. Also think of 'touch' as texture – what is the texture of the floor/jacket/tree bark? The more detailed the better!

Structure

Even though you're not writing a story, your description still needs structure. When planning your description, think of yourself as a cinematographer on a film – you get to choose what the reader 'sees'. You are doing a **one-shot take** but what will you show first and last? You may want to start with a **close-up** of a fallen soldier's face and **zoom out** to see the whole scene. Or perhaps going along a **single track**, taking in a beach crowded with hundreds of soldiers. Not all conflicts take place on land though; you could always take to the skies or space. Be creative and think like an Oscar-winner!

Spelling tip: 'el' and 'al' suffixes

The suffixes *al / el / le* can get confusing because they sound similar. For example, *principle / principal*. You could use the process of elimination. Try 'le' first as it's the most popular. The second most common is 'al'. You only use 'el' after the letters m, n, r, v, w.

Time to write

Write a description of a conflict zone.

Putting pen to paper

Now try one of the writing tasks below. Any of these tasks could be real or imagined circumstances.

1 Describe a time when you have felt fear.
2 Write a description of a person or an animal in pain.
3 Write a description of a hiding place.

Peer review (editing/drafting)

Reviewing your writing

Swap your writing with a partner. Read each other's work carefully, looking at:

- any uses of figurative language – are they effective?
- the way ideas are expressed – are they clear?
- how the description is structured – do the ideas link well?

Find two positive things that would improve the writing in your view. Share these with your partner.

Edit your work, considering these changes and correcting any spelling or punctuation errors.

Wider reading

If you want to read more about conflicts from across time and around the world, have a look at these brilliant books, which include poetry, graphic novels, fiction and non-fiction:

- *Poems from the First World War* (Published in Association with Imperial War Museums) selected by Gaby Morgan*
- *Cane Warriors* by Alex Wheatle*
- *Maus* by Art Spiegelman*
- *Carrie's War* by Nina Bawden
- *Girl on a Plane* by Miriam Moss*
- *Oranges in No Man's Land* by Elizabeth Laird
- *Never Fall Down* by Patricia McCormick*
- *Now or Never: A Dunkirk Story* by Bali Rai
- *All the Light We Cannot See* by Anthony Doerr*

*Choose these titles for a more challenging read!

Book review

Sum up a book you have read recently in ten words, then five and, finally, one word. It might be one from the wider reading list above.

Read your words to a partner. Are they intrigued? Does it make them want to read the book?

10 Loud and proud

- **Reading focus**: Making links to context and implied meaning
- **Writing focus**: Persuasive speeches
- **Speaking and listening focus**: Using body language and eye contact effectively
- **Language focus**: Persuasive language, direct address, free verse and sensory description, verb tenses
- **Drama focus**: Status

Context

Activism has always been around in many different forms but in the last few years has become more prominent than ever. Whether it's Greta Thunberg's climate strikes or Black Lives Matter protests or the Women's March, more and more people are making themselves heard by speaking out and it's important we listen. Whatever your beliefs, it's vital to hear all sides of an argument or issue to get the full picture so, even though the extracts in this chapter are about speaking out, they are not the complete picture, so read around an issue if you want more information. Don't stop here!

In this chapter, we will be reading how writers have been getting in on the act for a long time. We will read speeches and poetry that deliver a strong message about inequality, loudly and proudly. We will also read fiction which has opened many readers' eyes through minority characters, new points of view and unusual situations. All of this will culminate in writing your own persuasive speech on an issue you feel passionate about.

About the author

Jewell Parker Rhodes
is an American novelist
and educator. She has
written many books, for
both children and adults,
in which she hopes to
inspire social justice,
equality and care for
the environment.

Jerome is twelve years
old when he is shot by
a police officer. *Ghost
Boys* (2018) tells Jerome's
story from his point of
view when he was alive
and after he died. In this
extract, Jerome watches
the preliminary hearing
about his death.

Ghost Boys

It's April. I'm four months dead.

In the courthouse, I feel clammy and cold. Not weather cold, just empty cold. I'm stuck. Stuck in time. Stuck being dead.

5 Ma, Grandma and Pop are in the courtroom's front row behind the prosecutor. Reporters, sketch artists, Reverend Thornton, officers, and the community folks fill the rest of the seats. Right behind the lawyer's desk are a white woman and a girl, her daughter, maybe. Both have sandy-brown hair. Both look sad.

There's no jury – just empty seats.

10 The judge isn't tall, about the same height as my ma. She wears black shoes. Her nails are painted pink.

'Preliminary hearings,' she says, 'don't determine innocence or guilt. They determine whether there is enough evidence for a trial. Whether Officer Moore should be charged with murder.'

15 Seems lame to me. I'm dead, aren't I?

A policeman is sitting in the dock, below the judge's chair. He has sandy-brown hair, too. Glazed, blue eyes. A lawyer is saying something to him but he's not listening, just looking at the woman and the girl. His family, I think.

20 'Officer Moore, can you answer the question?'

'Sir?' the officer looks at the slim man.

'Were you in fear of your life?'

'Yes, yes. He had a gun.'

'Were you surprised later when the gun turned out to be a toy?'

25 'Yes. It looked real. He was threatening me.'

I shake my head. I never pointed a gun at the policeman. I walk closer to the officer. *Why's he telling lies?*

The girl in the front row points at me, whispers to her mother. I look at the girl, her eyes wide with fear. Like her dad was scared of me?

30 Her mother shushes her. Shoves her hand down.

The prosecutor continues, 'How old was the assailant?'

'I thought at least twenty-five. He was a man. A dangerous man.'

'So you were doing your job as trained?'

'Yes.'

35 'Were you upset to discover the man was a boy? A twelve-year-old boy?'

Ma starts moaning, crying, soft yet sharp.

'I was surprised. He was big, hulking. Scary.'

'You felt threatened?'

The officer pauses. I'm staring right into his eyes. He looks through 40 me. He's studying his wife and daughter. His daughter is studying me. I don't know why or how she sees me.

He swallows, his tongue licking his bottom lip. 'I…felt…threatened.'

Pop stands, shouting, 'A grown man. Two grown men. You. Your partner, Officer Whitter. Armed. Threatened by a boy?'

45 Ma wails.

The judge pounds her gavel. 'Quiet. Quiet in the courtroom.'

'Black lives matter!' someone hollers.

'Jerome mattered,' shouts Grandma. 'He was a good boy.'

Jewell Parker Rhodes

Questions

1 How long has it been since Jerome died? (1)
2 What colour hair do the white woman, girl and police officer have? (1)
3 The judge's nails are painted red. True or false? (1) **FP**
4 Officer Moore thought Jerome was carrying a gun. What was he actually carrying? (1)
5 Who is Officer Moore's work partner? (1)

Grammar focus
No tension with tense

Even though Jerome is 'stuck in the past' you'll notice he narrates in the present. Telling a narrative from multiple perspectives or from multiple time periods may require a careful use of different **tenses**. But, in general, your aim should be to maintain the same tense throughout your writing. Thinking of tenses on a timeline can really help:

Past ———————— Present ———————— Future ————————

Once you've decided on the tense you're going to write in, focus on using that verb tense consistently. You'll notice you don't have to change much else to time-travel in tense!

Draw the timeline above and write these sentences in different tenses, placing them on the timeline in the correct place:

I sit in the courtroom   *She watches her father*   *They shout*

About the author

Catherine Bruton is a British author and also an English teacher. She writes about subjects that her pupils are impacted by such as terrorism, celebrity and immigration.

No Ballet Shoes in Syria (2019) charts the life of Aya and her family as they adjust to life in Britain after a terrifying ordeal in war-torn Aleppo and the subsequent journey to safety. In this extract, Aya is dancing in a car park outside a community centre when Miss Helena, a formidable ballet teacher, spots her and her potential.

1 The mass of silky, feathery plumed seeds produced by a thistle.

No Ballet Shoes in Syria

Aya let the emotions take her now. The music sped up and she leapt, air-bound, hands shooting upwards towards the white sky, then plummeting low to the weed-strewn ground.

The memories rushed in…border guards…the refugee camp…the airless
5 *container…the boat across the sea…the storm…*

She spun again – one, two, three times.

The sea…the boat…the beach…blood in the water…

Her body jerked to a stop. No – there were things she couldn't allow herself to remember.

10 'Sometimes the only thing you can do is dance, isn't it?'

Aya lurched back into the present. She felt dizzy and dazed, and it took her a second to reconnect with where she was.

Standing at the top of the metal staircase was the tiny old dance teacher. Today she was dressed in a long purple skirt and giant grey
15 knitted cardigan that swept nearly to her ankles. She looked even more like an ancient fairy queen – skin papery, eyes two violets, hair like thistledown[1].

'You feel the music in here.' The old lady tapped her own chest as she made her way carefully down the metal staircase, watching
20 Aya intently.

Aya was breathless and dizzy, still taking in the red-brick walls, the wheelie bins, the rusted railing… For a few moments she'd been back in Aleppo.

'I saw you watching my class the other day.'

Aya felt herself stiffen. 'I'm sorry – I –'

25 The old lady waved her hand dismissively. 'You have been trained where?'

'Trained?' She realised she'd become used to mistrusting people – it was a hard habit to break.

The old lady was looking her up and down with a critical, self-appraising eye that made Aya feel stiff and self-conscious.

30 'Which ballet school did you go to?'

'I – don't. We've just arrived. In England. Three weeks.'

'Three weeks. And before that?'

Aya thought of the list of places they had travelled through. She remembered Dad counting them off on his long brown fingers and
35 laughing: Syria, camp at Kilis, across the sea from Izmir, to Greece – the beach on Chios – all the way to England. 'Our Grand Tour,' he had called it. Only Dad could have made fleeing their home seem like an adventure.

'Aleppo,' Aya said quietly.

'I see.' The old lady seemed to comprehend something and she nodded.
40 'Sometimes it seems that the world never learns.'

The sun had come out through the white blanket of cloud, making even the dirty red brick take on a brighter hue.

'I – I do not understand.'

'No, of course you don't.' The old lady's eyes traced Aya's features, and
45 for the second time in two days, she felt that somebody was really looking at her – not through her.

'Perhaps,' said the old lady quietly, 'you would be liking to join my dance class upstairs?'

Aya felt herself flush. 'You said there is no space…'

50 'For the right dancers, we can always find a little more space, I think.'

Hot steam belched out of a pipe, giving off a smell of stewed meat and carrots. Aya's stomach rumbled and she realised how hungry she was. She looked down at her feet and shrugged. 'I…we have no money – to pay. For the lessons.'

55 The old lady moved slowly down the last steps, her eyes intently on Aya.

'When I first came to England,' she said, glancing around at the weeds and the cigarette butts, 'I relied a great deal on the kindness of strangers – as somebody once said. I forget who.'

Catherine Bruton

Questions

1 What is Miss Helena wearing today? (2)
2 What did Aya's Dad call their journey from Syria to England? (1)
3 What language technique is used in 'white blanket of cloud' (line 41)? (1)
4 What does the word 'traced' (line 44) mean? (1) FP
    a examined   c drew
    b discovered   d covered
5 What did Miss Helena rely on when she first came to England? (1)

Punctuation tip: apostrophes for possession

If the subject **possesses** the object, you need a **possessive** apostrophe.

For example: *The dog's bone* or *Jerome's toy*.

And you still need one if the subject is plural or has a 's' at the end of the word, just in a different place.

For example: *The dogs' bones* or *Thomas' room*.

Talking point

As a small group, read through some recent newspapers or watch a news bulletin relating to issues of inequality. Discuss the following points once you've finished reading, giving everyone a chance to share their opinions:

- What report resonated with you the most and why?
- Explain the points of view in the story. For example, were experts asked for their opinion, were eyewitnesses or the subjects interviewed?
- What other questions do you have about the issue explored?

Did you spot any similarities within the stories you chose or your ideas about them? We're all different so we can react to things in different ways; it's important to acknowledge that so we can learn from others.

Writing questions on *Ghost Boys*

1 In what ways has the author created a distinct character voice for Jerome? (4)
2 What is your impression of Officer Moore? (2)
3 Do you think Officer Moore is telling the truth? Use evidence to support your ideas. (3)
4 Comment on the girl's reaction to Jerome. (2)

Writing questions on *No Ballet Shoes in Syria*

1 What is the effect of the punctuation in lines 4–7? (4)
2 What is your impression of Aya? (4)
3 What is the community centre like? How can you tell? (4)
4 In your own words, explain what Aya feels by the phrase 'she felt that somebody was really looking at her – not through her' (lines 45–46). (3)

Speaking and listening focus
Body language

Non-verbal communication is just as important as what you say, especially when it comes to public speaking.

In pairs, you are going to play emotion charades. Without any sound, you will have 30 seconds to show your partner how you feel by reacting to different situations through only your facial expressions and body language. Your partner must then guess the emotion and situation you're portraying. Make sure you keep eye contact too, because you only have three guesses and the eyes will help reveal the answer.

Use the emotional situations below as a starting point but feel free to make up your own:

> You are giving a speech to a large audience and it goes well
> *(nervous / focused / confident / overjoyed).*

> You find a snake in your wardrobe
> *(relaxed / surprised / terrified / thrilled).*

> You are nominated for an award but someone else wins
> *(excited / anticipation / disappointed / resigned).*

Thematic focus

Even though these extracts are set in very different circumstances, the characters are both suffering injustices. Focusing on the characters, complete the table below using quotes from the extracts (we have started one for you).

Characters	How they're described	What they say and how they say it	The actions they take
Jerome	Officer says he looks older than he is	First person narrator	Steps towards officer and stares at him but has no effect

What stands out to you? Do the characters in different books have more in common than you thought? Share your findings and thoughts in a small group, then add them to your notes.

Extended writing questions

You will now be writing an extended answer about an extract. Write your answer in three PEEA paragraphs, using evidence from the text to support your ideas. (See page 179 in the Exam skills chapter for an explanation of the PEEA technique.)

Here are some tips for writing extended answers:

- Read the questions carefully.
- Use the three foci in your topic sentences for the three paragraphs.
- It might help you to find your evidence for each before you start writing.
- Use connectives like 'and', 'furthermore', 'however' and 'additionally' to expand your explanations.

1   How does the author create a sense of drama in Extract 1 from *Ghost Boys*?

    You should focus on narrative perspective, dialogue and structure.

OR

2   How does the author make Miss Helena a memorable and significant character in Extract 2 from *No Ballet Shoes in Syria*?

    You should focus on description, the character's actions and dialogue.

OR

3   Write a letter as Aya to a friend she used to dance with. Explore how she has been feeling, what happened when she met Miss Helena and what she expects will happen now.

Language focus
Meaning through context

Writers can be sneaky. Instead of saying something directly, they can suggest or hint at something – this is called **implied meaning**. Where there is implied meaning, a reader has to use their inference skills to understand. Remember: the writer implies; the reader infers. It's like being bored but, instead of saying so, looking at your watch and yawning.

In this book, we have looked at many ways in which meaning is implied, such as imagery and how characters speak. But another strategy is thinking about the context of the text. Here are some questions to ask yourself about the texts that you read:

- When was it written or set (historical context)?
- What was happening at the time it was written or set (social context)?
- Who wrote it (author)?
- Who is it written for (audience)?
- Why was it written (purpose)?

About the author

Dean Atta is a British poet of Greek Cypriot and Caribbean descent. His poetry often explores identity and social justice. He has been commissioned by a variety of museums and art galleries.

The Black Flamingo (2019) is a novel-in-verse about a mixed-race gay teen who struggles with his identity. In this poem, an image of a flamingo is used to explain how conflicted the character is feeling. Discuss the questions in the boxes with a partner.

1 What are the connotations of the colour pink?

2 What is a synonym for 'hue'?

3 When you think of flamingos, do you think of 'blending in'?

6 In your own words, explain what the speaker wants more than anything.

8 How might knowing the context of this poem and the background of the poet help us understand the implied meaning?

'I Want to be a Pink Flamingo'

Pink. Definitely pink.[1]

I want my feathers to match

the hue[2] you imagine.

I want to blend in.

Nothing but Flamingoness.[3]

David Attenborough would say,

'Here we see the most typical flamingo.'[4]

Though I don't want to be the most,[5]

just typical. A wrapping-paper pattern.

I don't want to stand apart.[6]

Nothing different about my parts.

My beak just a beak, my head just a head.[7]

My neck, body, wings. Simply fit for purpose.

Standing on one leg, just like the rest.

Pink. Definitely pink.[8]

Dean Atta

4 When you've seen flamingos in pictures or documentaries, how do they act in a group?

5 Why does the speaker make this distinction?

7 What language technique is used?

Langston Hughes (1901–1967) was a central figure in the Harlem Renaissance (1920s) as a poet, novelist, columnist and playwright, but he was also a social activist for civil rights in America. He grew up in Ohio and gained a place at Columbia University in New York. He dropped out but publishers were already interested in his work and he eventually graduated from Lincoln University instead.

In this poem, Hughes' message is never explicit, but he implies the meaning through vivid imagery – people's right to live their dreams, whatever the colour of their skin.

Questions

1 Explain the meaning of 'deferred' (line 1). (1)
2 What language technique is used in 'dry up / like a raisin in the sun' (lines 2–3)? (1)
3 What is the definition of 'fester' (line 4) in this context? (1)
4 What language technique is used in lines 1, 3, 5, 6, 8 and 11 of the poem? (1)

'Harlem'

What happens to a dream deferred?

    Does it dry up
    like a raisin in the sun?
    Or fester like a sore—
5   And then run?
    Does it stink like rotten meat?
    Or crust and sugar over—
    like a syrupy sweet?

    Maybe it just sags
10   like a heavy load.

    Or does it explode?

Langston Hughes

Context

Langston Hughes was an activist, as well as a poet, so it's no surprise that his poetry contained calls for change. This poem was written in 1951, an era when racial segregation in America was still the norm and black people were victims of harsh racial discrimination across the world. Civil Rights protests began in earnest, calling for equality, but it was only the beginning of an ongoing struggle.

Research

There is a lot more to discover about Hughes and his contemporaries. Use the questions below to guide your own research:
- Where is Harlem and why do you think the poem is named after it?
- What other artists were made famous through the Harlem Renaissance?
- What famous acts have performed at the Apollo Theater in Harlem and when?
- Who were the key figures in the Civil Rights Movement in the USA during the 1960s?

Language focus
Use of senses

Sensory description is a powerful device to put a reader in the writer's or character's shoes. Describing what something looks like, smells like, sounds like, feels like or tastes like makes the description come to life. It can also make sense of something intangible, like an emotion, by comparing it to a physical sensation.

Hughes uses vivid sensory language in this poem. What connotations come to mind for 'fester' or 'stink' and 'crust'? Out-of-date food? Even the 'syrupy sweet' does not sound appealing because of the **sibilance** of the repeated 's'.

Research

The Civil Rights Movement in America caused ripples across the world, highlighting the inequalities between races. Learn more about how race relations in Britain were evolving using these research questions as a guide:
- What is the significance of Windrush?
- What were the uprisings in 1958 in London and Nottingham about?
- When did the Notting Hill Carnival begin? Who started it and why?

Writing questions on 'Harlem'

1 What does Hughes mean by 'a dream deferred' (line 1)? (2)
2 Choose two similes from the poem and explain their effect. (4)
3 What do you notice about the structure of this poem? What effect was the poet trying to create? (3)
4 Why do you think the last line is italicised? (2)

Text features
Structure and form

'Harlem' has a unique structure. You may have spotted an ABCBDED rhyme scheme in the middle section, but the majority is written in **free verse**. It doesn't have a consistent or regular rhythm or rhyme and just follows the patterns of natural speech.

The shape the poem takes is unusual too, with the first and last lines standing alone from the rest. Try to link the meaning of this poem to its structure.

About the author

As a UN Women Goodwill Ambassador, this speaker delivered this speech for the HeForShe campaign at the United Nations Headquarters in New York on 20 September 2014.

'Gender Equality is Your Issue Too'

I am reaching out to you because I need your help. We want to end gender inequality—and to do that we need everyone to be involved...

I was appointed six months ago and the more I have spoken about feminism the more I have realized that fighting for women's rights has too often become synonymous with man-hating. If there is one thing I know for certain, it is that this has to stop.

For the record, feminism by definition is: 'The belief that men and women should have equal rights and opportunities. It is the theory of the political, economic and social equality of the sexes.'

I started questioning gender-based assumptions when at eight I was confused at being called 'bossy', because I wanted to direct the plays we would put on for our parents—but the boys were not.

When at 14 I started being sexualized by certain elements of the press.

When at 15 my girlfriends started dropping out of their sports teams because they didn't want to appear 'muscly'.

When at 18 my male friends were unable to express their feelings.

I decided I was a feminist, and this seemed uncomplicated to me. But my recent research has shown me that feminism[1] has become an unpopular word...

Why is the word such an uncomfortable one?

I am from Britain and think it is right that as a woman I am paid the same as my male counterparts. I think it is right that I should be able to make decisions about my own body. I think it is right that women be involved on my behalf in the policies and decision-making of my country. I think it is right that socially I am afforded the same respect as men. But sadly, I can say that there is no one country in the world where all women can expect to receive these rights.

No country in the world can yet say they have achieved gender equality...

And if you still hate the word—it is not the word that is important but the idea and the ambition behind it. Because not all women have been afforded the same rights that I have. In fact, statistically, very few have been.

In 1995, Hilary Clinton made a famous speech in Beijing about women's rights. Sadly, many of the things she wanted to change are still a reality today.

But what stood out for me the most was that only 30 per cent of her audience were male. How can we affect change in the world when only half of it is invited or feel welcome to participate in the conversation?

Men—I would like to take this opportunity to extend your formal invitation. Gender equality is your issue too.

1   The belief that women should be allowed the same rights, power and opportunities as men and be treated in the same way.

Questions

1   In your own words, what is the HeforShe campaign's aim? (3)
2   What is the effect of the speaker using examples from her personal experience? Refer to evidence from the text to support your ideas. (4)
3   What year did Hilary Clinton give her famous speech in Beijing? (1)
4   In the context of the text, what does 'distorted' (line 46) mean? (1)
5   Read lines 51–52. What two things should both men and women feel? (2)

2   Take on certain responsibilities and opportunities from someone else. A mantle is an old word for a cloak.

Because to date, I've seen my father's role as a parent being valued less by society despite my needing his presence as a child as much as my mother's.

45   I've seen young men suffering from mental illness unable to ask for help for fear it would make them look less 'macho'... I've seen men made fragile and insecure by a distorted sense of what constitutes male success. Men don't have the benefits of equality either.

We don't often talk about men being imprisoned by gender stereotypes but I can see that that they are and that when they are free, things will

50   change for women as a natural consequence...

Both men and women should feel free to be sensitive. Both men and women should feel free to be strong.

If we stop defining each other by what we are not and start defining ourselves by what we are—we can all be freer...

55   I want men to take up this mantle[2]. So their daughters, sisters and mothers can be free from prejudice but also so that their sons have permission to be vulnerable and human too...

You might be thinking, who is this girl? And what is she doing up on stage at the UN? It's a good question and trust me, I have been asking

60   myself the same thing. I don't know if I am qualified to be here. All I know is that I care about this problem. And I want to make it better.

Text features

Personal becomes persuasive

Using personal experience or an **anecdote** in a speech can help make your points more relevant to and engaging for the audience. All of a sudden, the person at the podium is just like you! It's a persuasive technique too – it's a real-life authentic example of the point you're trying to make.

In her speech, the speaker uses personal experience as a structural device in lines 10–15 by listing the ages when she suffered from inequalities. She also refers to a past stage in the debate when she mentions Hilary Clinton's Beijing speech. By using specific ages and dates, the points feel more convincing.

Read more

Search for Malala Yousafzai's sixteenth birthday UN speech about education. Notice how she uses personal experience and direct address to engage the delegates.

Research

Interested to know more about the fight for gender equality? Use the questions below to guide your own research on the topic:

- 'Women's rights are human rights' – watch Hilary Clinton's 1995 Beijing women's speech. Are there parts that resonate with you?
- What are the aims of UN Women and what does it do to achieve them?
- When and why was the United Nations formed?

Language focus
I'm talking to you!

The speaker on page 168 uses **first person perspective** effectively in this speech. But it's not all about her.

If you look closely, she uses **collective nouns**, such as 'we', which create unity with the listener and a sense of purpose as a team.

She also uses **direct address**, which isn't as subtle but just as impactful. For example, 'Men – I would like to take this opportunity to extend your formal invitation.' In this case, listeners are spoken to directly, involving them in the speech. It gets their attention and, because it can sometimes feel accusatory, makes them question their involvement with the issue or why they haven't engaged with the issue already.

 # Drama focus
High or low?

Without any sound, walk around the room as a high-status character. What defines high-status body language? Now try low-status. How has your body language changed? In pairs, interact as high- and low-status characters. How do you interact with each other physically? How do you feel in both statuses? Using this as inspiration, create a scene between you that features characters of different status.

Writing task

When writing a speech, it's important to remember that it won't just be **read** but also it will be **heard**. You are going to write your own **persuasive speech** on an issue you feel passionate about.

Your first task is to choose that issue. It might be inspired by one of the extracts in this chapter or something you've read in a newspaper or seen on a news bulletin. Make it relevant to you and your peers.

Your second task is to do your detailed research. As you've seen, using specific facts and data is really persuasive.

You may want to practise planning with key phrases or topic sentences using the following persuasive devices which were also covered in the Our planet chapter:

> **A**lliteration – alliterative phrases are catchy and stick in a listener's mind.
>
> **A**necdote – a short, personal story makes your point relevant to a listener.

Look back at page 135 in the Different people, different perspectives chapter for more information about anecdotes.

> Counter-**A**rgument – acknowledge the other side of the argument but then quash it.
>
> **F**acts – clear, true facts add credibility to your ideas.
>
> **O**pinions – your opinions or others', such as witnesses or experts.
>
> **R**hetorical questions – make the listener question their own culpability, or use them to structure your argument.
>
> **R**epetition – emphasises a point.
>
> **E**motive language – vocabulary or imagery that creates emotion.
>
> **S**tatistics – percentages or numbers add credibility to your ideas.
>
> **T**riplets – a sentence made up of a list of three is memorable and impactful.

An easy way to remember these is the mnemonic **AFORREST**.

Use the planning sheet shown opposite to write your own persuasive speech on an issue you feel passionate about.

Although you will spend more time on your own views in this speech, be respectful of the opposing viewpoint. You don't know what your reader's or listener's view will be and you want them to stay engaged so they can be persuaded.

Introduction

What is the issue? What is your point of view?

_____

You need to make three to four clear and different points, with evidence, using persuasive devices:

Point 1:

_____

Evidence:

_____

Point 2:

_____

Evidence

_____

Point 3 (include a counter-argument):

_____

Evidence:

_____

Point 4:

_____

Evidence:

_____

Conclusion

Summarise your point of view. Use a final punchy statement or rhetorical question to stick in the reader's or listener's mind.

_____

Spelling tip: 'there', 'their' and 'they're'

there (showing position)
their (showing ownership)
they're (contraction of 'they are')

Double check which one you need by checking its function.

Time to write

Write your own persuasive speech on an issue you feel passionate about.

Putting pen to paper

Now try one of the writing tasks below. You may want to do some of your own research before starting your piece.

1   Write a speech persuading your teachers to give you less homework.
2   Write a speech persuading your parents to give you more pocket money.
3   Write a speech about why school uniform should be banned.

Peer review

Reviewing your writing

Swap your writing with a partner. Read each other's work carefully, looking at:

- the use of persuasive language features from the list on page 172 – are they used effectively?
- the way ideas are expressed – are they clear?
- how the speech is structured – do the ideas link well?

Finally, read your speech aloud, considering your body language and maintaining eye contact with your audience – does this change your partner's view of it in any way? Listen closely to your partner's speech.

Find two positive things that would improve the writing in your view. Share these with your partner.

Edit your work, considering these changes and correcting any spelling or punctuation errors.

> ### Wider reading
>
> If you enjoyed the extracts in this chapter, have a look at these brilliant books and fantastic writers:
>
> - *Roll of Thunder Hear My Cry* by Mildred D Taylor*
> - *Anita and Me* by Meera Syal
> - *Poetry for Young People* by Maya Angelou*
> - *Things a Bright Girl Can Do* by Sally Nicholls
> - *The Crossover* by Kwame Alexander
> - *Cocoa Girl* magazine
> - the writings of Juno Dawson
> - *Nothing but the Truth* by Dick Lehr*
> - *I Am Malala* by Malala Yousafzai*
>
> *Choose these titles for a more challenging read!

Book review

Prepare a short review for a book you have read recently. It might be one from the wider reading list above.

Remember to include three things about your chosen book which made you want to read on.

Share your review with a partner. What do you think of their book recommendation?

Reading skills

In the reading exam you will asked to read a comprehension text which may be in the form of **prose**, **drama** or **poetry**. Pay attention to the chosen form as it will make a difference to how you answer the questions. For example, for a drama text it will be important to remember that it's meant to be performed.

Remember that comprehension means 'understanding' so take your time to read the text carefully. Read it once to comprehend and then look at the questions; then you can do a second informed reading because you know what you're looking for.

Short reading response question

The first set of questions you will answer will be multiple-choice questions, which may seem easy, but you must be able to spot red herrings. In some cases, it will be about picking the best answer, not just the right answer. The question will often refer to a particular line or section and you will have to circle your answer. Each question will be worth 1 or 2 marks.

Look at these sample questions and read the explanations beneath to see how best to approach each type of question.

Literal meaning questions

Where is most of the scene set?

- a a forest
- b a house
- c a beach
- d a garden

This is a **literal** question, meaning the answer can be found in the text (as this is a drama text, it's probably in the stage directions) but there are several answers which are similar. The question says the 'most of the scene' so it's possible the scene moves between settings too. Read the question carefully. Double checking your answers is important here.

You can find the answer in the *Noughts and Crosses* extract on page 74.

The answer is: c   a beach

Tips for improving

On first reading a text, look for key information (names, places, times) which you can recall later. You may also want to practise **scanning** texts for information – this is vital in literal questions.

Implied meaning questions

Read lines 25–28. What adjective best describes how Mr Laurence feels?

a angry
b calm
c worried
d upset

This question requires you to read between the lines to see nuances in meaning and choose the best answer.

You can find the answer in the *Little Women* extract on page 126.

The answer is: c   worried

Tips for improving

Take notice of the lines and re-read them carefully for clues. In these lines, Mr Laurence is pacing the room and the simile describing how he would rather face an army than Beth's mother helps the reader understand he is worried above all.

Grammar questions

Which of these lines from the poem is a complete sentence?

a Nothing gold can stay.
b But only so an hour.
c Her early leaf's a flower;
d So Eden sank to grief,

This question is testing your **grammatical** knowledge rather than your knowledge about the poem. Watch out for these types of questions because, as usual, small details make a big difference and you don't want to miss something.

You can find the answer in the poem 'Nothing Gold Can Stay' on page 17.

The answer is: a   Nothing gold can stay.

Tips for improving

Get confident with key grammar rules. In this case, you had to spot not only the full stop but also that the line has a verb and subject, which makes it a complete sentence.

Look further on in this chapter for more grammar rule reminders.

Some of you will take a version of the reading exam in which you will come across some different question types as well as the ones above. You will only answer questions on a **prose** passage, rather than another form.

Find information questions

These questions will ask you to choose the correct answer from a list or ask you which answer in the list is true or false. They are checking to see that you can find information in the text.

Tips for improving

Check all the answers carefully. Sometimes your first instinct can be right but a slight change in wording or spelling might distract you from the right answer.

Sample question

Which one of these statements is true?

a   The narrator's name is Melanie.
b   The narrator's name is Melody.
c   The narrator's name is Melissa.
d   The narrator's name is Melinda.

You can find the answer in the extract from *Out of my Mind* on page 124.

The answer is: b   The narrator's name is Melody.

'This means' questions

These questions want to check that you have understood what you have read so they will give you different options for what something means. You must pick the best answer.

Tips for improving

If you are not sure what a word means or not sure what the answer is immediately, use the process of elimination to cut down your options before choosing.

Sample question

Aya feels 'stiff and self-conscious' when Miss Helena looks at her. This means:

a   she is relaxed and at ease
b   she is still and thinking
c   she is tense and aware of herself
d   she is tall and uncomfortable.

You can find the answer in the extract from *No Ballet Shoes in Syria* on page 160.

The answer is: c   she is tense and aware of herself

Rewrite questions

These questions are testing your spelling, punctuation and grammar, as well as understanding, by rewriting part of the text.

Tips for improving

You might spot the errors immediately but remember to proofread by comparing your answer to the original to double check you noticed everything.

Sample question

Rewrite the following sentences without the apostrophes and filling in the omitted letters:

'The fever's turned, she's sleepin' nat'ral, her skin's damp, and she breathes easy. Praise be given! Oh, my goodness me!'

You can find the answer in the *Little Women* extract on page 126.

The answer is:

'The fever has turned, she is sleeping natural, her skin is damp, and she breathes easy. Praise be given! Oh, my goodness me!'

Unlocking a poem

The way you read a poem can help unlock its meaning to you, even before you look at the questions. A poem is usually a shorter amount of text than prose fiction or a drama script, but it is packed with meaning. Luckily, because it's shorter, you have a chance to read it multiple times. Follow the reading steps to get the most out of this poem:

1 Read the title
It seems simple but is easy to forget. 'Anthem' means an 'uplifting' song like the National Anthem and contrasts with 'Doomed Youth', meaning the 'tragic, inevitable death of young people'.

4 Read for structure
The third time you read through, pay close attention to the punctuation and any changes of mood. The dashes and caesura in this poem emphasise key moments by slowing down the reader. Questions are asked of us too, making us feel involved.

2 Read to comprehend
Gain an understanding of what the poem is about. On this first read you might pick out words you don't know, such as 'orisons' and 'pall' to revisit later.

'Anthem for Doomed Youth'[1]

What passing-bells for these who die as cattle?[3]

[4] — Only the monstrous anger of the guns.[3]

Only the stuttering rifles' rapid rattle[3]

Can patter out their hasty orisons.[2]

No mockeries now for them;[4] no prayers nor bells;

Nor any voice of mourning save the choirs,—

The shrill, demented choirs of wailing shells[3];

And bugles calling for them from sad shires.[3]

What candles may be held to speed them all?[3]

Not in the hands of boys, but in their eyes

Shall shine the holy glimmers of goodbyes.[3]

The pallor of girls' brows shall be their pall;[2]

Their flowers the tenderness of patient minds,

And each slow dusk a drawing-down of blinds.[3]

Wilfred Owen

3 Read for imagery
On this second read, identify language techniques and effective vocabulary. In this poem, people are compared to animals, personification brings weapons to life and alliteration and assonance are used to create the sounds of battle.

How to PEEA

You do not get marks for writing in a PEEA paragraph structure, but you will get marks for the clarity and content of your answer. PEEA is a great way to get both those things so it's worth using.

Read the annotated example below and use the structure for PEEAs of your own.

1 Point – answer the question in one sentence using words from the question.

2 Evidence – a quotation from the text or close reference embedded in a sentence.

3 Identify techniques and use terminology when you can.

4 Explanation – the longest part and worth the most marks.

The imagery used to describe the battlefield also suggests anger.[1] This is evident in 'the monstrous anger of the guns'.[2] The poet uses personification[3] to bring the weapons to life by giving the guns a negative human emotion. The effect of this is that the guns seem to have a mind of their own because they act in anger.[4] Additionally,[5] by using the verb 'monstrous'[6] the poet shows how strong the anger is, so much so that it's compared to a monster.[7]

6 Single word analysis.

7 More detail added to the analysis.

5 Signpost word extends your explanation to analysis.

Signposting PEEA answers

Here are some sentence starters to help you get going with the different sections within PEEA:

Point	Evidence	Explanation/Analysis
The character...	This is evident in...	This suggests that...
The author uses...	For example...	This implies that...
The writer creates a...	The evidence for this is...	The effect of...
		This is significant because...
		In addition...
		Furthermore...

Longer reading response questions

The next set of questions you answer in the exam will require inference about characters and analysis of language, as well as summarising. This questions in this section are worth between 4 and 8 marks.

Look at these sample question types and read the explanations beneath to see how best to approach them.

Language question

In this **language question**, you deal with the answer in two sections. Label each section clearly when you answer it. Name any language techniques you identify in the quotes to show what you know.

Tips for improving

Using single word analysis helps extend your explanations but also strengthen them by reinforcing your point. It gives you a chance to use more terminology (in this case an adjective) too.

Sample question

a   Find two quotations that describe the berries positively.
b   Explain how the poet suggests the berries are delicious.

You can find the answer in the poem 'Blackberry Picking' on page 18.

One **possible answer** might include:

a   'its flesh was sweet / Like thickened wine'
b   *The quotation illustrates how the poet suggests the berries are delicious through a simile. The poet compares the berries to sweet wine, which implies they taste sweet and rich. Using the adjective 'thickened' suggests that the taste is full and syrupy, which makes the experience even more pleasant.*

Context questions using summary

This **contextual question** requires you to explain the quotation in your own words. As it says, 'in the context of the poem', you will also have to summarise what is happening in the poem to link its meaning to the poem. The question is worth 4 marks, so 2 marks for explaining the meaning and 2 marks for linking to your understanding of the whole poem.

Sample question

Explain the meaning of this line in the context of the poem:

'Good pilgrim, you do wrong your hand too much'

You can find the answer in the extract from *Romeo and Juliet* on page 82.

One **possible answer** might be:

In this quote, by continuing the image of their hands kissing when they touch, Juliet says to Romeo that he has gone too far by trying to kiss her.

Tips for improving

Look carefully at the marks – they tell you how much to write. In summaries, compare the marks to the key words in the quote and focus on them accordingly.

Questions using inference

This question requires information about a character. You should write in a PEEA structure, which means a distinct point, evidence and analysis about that character.

Sample question

What is your impression of Miss Havisham in this extract?

You can find the answer in the extract from *Great Expectations* on page 12.

One **possible answer** might include:

Miss Havisham is manipulative. This is suggested in the repeated question, 'Anything else?' She says this repeatedly to Pip, a young boy who is in a vulnerable position, about Estella. It is as if she is trying to get an answer she wants and it shows she controls this situation, as well as the children's feelings and actions.

Tips for improving

Keep your answer structure simple by using PEEA. Aim for one sentence per section.

Explain questions

These questions need slightly longer answers so using a PEEA structure will help, but the focus of the mark scheme is the explanation.

Sample question

Explain how Callum feels about Sephy.

You can find the answer in the extract from *Noughts and Crosses* on page 74.

One **possible answer** might include:

Callum clearly has romantic feelings for Sephy. This is evident in his words 'shock like static electricity zapped through my body.' This suggests he is reacting physically to seeing her and that the attraction he describes through the simile is like a tingling, and is pleasant. Even though later he becomes angry with Sephy, this is still due to his intense feelings for her.

Tips for improving

Always include an 'and' in your explanation – this will ensure you're writing as much as possible.

Extended reading response questions

In response to the final question in your reading exam, you will be writing an extended answer of around three PEEA paragraphs. That might seem like a lot but don't panic! You will develop a logical argument based on the question that covers the whole text (it might be about a theme, for example). Here are some tips for approaching an extended response question:

- Firstly, read the question carefully and look for the key words. Use these key words to form your topic sentences / points for each paragraph.
- Another good strategy is to find the evidence first and build around it. Make sure the quotations you choose have enough scope for analysis.
- Using single word analysis will help you develop your explanations too, because to get the top marks you will need to provide deeper analysis and discussion of language.
- Use signpost words and phrases, like 'furthermore' and 'in addition' to expand your explanations.

It is important to discuss the text imaginatively, perhaps looking at the question in a different way, while staying focused on the question and the evidence you choose from the text.

Here's an example of this type of question:

Sample question

How does the author create a sense of anger in the extract?

You should consider structure, imagery and vocabulary in your answer.

You can find the answer in the extract from 'Anthem for Doomed Youth' on page 178.

One **possible answer** might be:

The author creates a sense of anger in the speaker's tone by using rhetorical questions at the beginning of each stanza. An example of this is 'What candles may be held to speed them all?' Rhetorical questions are questions that require no answer and instead make the reader think. The questions in the poem are directed to the reader by the speaker who is exasperated and looking for answers.

The imagery used to describe the battlefield also suggests anger. This is evident in 'the monstrous anger of the guns'. The poet uses personification to bring the weapons to life by giving the guns a human emotion. The effect of this is that the guns seem to have a mind of their own because they act in anger. Additionally, by using the verb 'monstrous' the poet shows how strong the anger is, so much so that it's compared to a monster.

A range of vocabulary is used to show the speaker's anger at the wasteful death of the soldiers but the repetition of the negatives 'not', 'no' and 'nor' are very effective. By repeating these adverbs and conjunction, the negative tone is evident throughout the poem and emphasises the lack of respect the soldiers will be shown in death.

Tips for improving

Avoid repetition or overlapping of your ideas and use different quotations and make distinct points.

Directed writing question in response to reading

These extended questions are there to demonstrate your empathy skills and your imagination while using the information from the extract. You will be given a task, which you must adhere to, and then three bullet points, which you can potentially form three paragraphs from if it works for the task.

Sample question

Retell the story from Estella's point of view.

You should explore:

- her observations of Pip
- her feelings about Miss Havisham
- whether she would like to see Pip again or not.

You can find the answer in the extract from *Great Expectations* on page 12.

One **possible answer** might be:

What type of a name is Pip? A pip is what you find in an apple: small, brown and disgusting. On the other hand, it is a seed too. I wonder what this coarse little boy will grow into. I doubt it will be a fine apple tree or an oak or fir tree; he will probably be a weed. Especially with those manners and those card skills. And don't get me started on his clothes!

I cannot begin to think why Miss Havisham should invite him over to play cards when he has no experience whatsoever. The game was so easily won, I learnt nothing from him. I do wonder if it was all for her own amusement. To see me so annoyed and that silly boy all flushed and awkward. Maybe she is just bored of me, of sitting here day after day. She needed a distraction. I certainly wish I did not have to be involved with her stupid games.

But the games will continue as that boy is coming back. I heard them whispering. I'd much rather not see this Pip boy again. We have nothing in common and it all seems like a waste of my time. I guess I could teach him how to play cards properly and then at last I could have a decent game with someone.

Tips for improving

Use details from the text to show you have understood the extract, as well as to gain more ideas for your answer.

For more practise of this type of question, look at the extended writing questions in each of Chapters 1 to 10.

Writing skills

In the writing exam, you will choose two options from a choice of four, which may include: narrative writing; a descriptive piece or report on a journey, event or person; a persuasive speech; a letter discussing an issue and making recommendations to the reader. Each option is worth 50 marks.

They will be based on different topics and situations, as well as having different purposes. Getting to know the requirements of those purposes and knowing the text types you feel most confident with ahead of the exam would be really helpful.

You can choose whichever tasks you like but you might want to choose different text types to show off what you can do. Tasks you feel most confident with and topics you feel passionate about will be good choices, so you do not waste time agonising over what to write or how.

Talking of which, you have 30 minutes to write each piece plus 15 minutes to choose the tasks, plan and proofread. Use all the time because there is a lot to do, but manage your time and you'll be fine!

Advice writing tasks

You may be asked to write a letter giving recommendations in the exam. In this case you are being asked to advise the recipient of the letter. When writing to advise, always moderate your tone and respect the recipient's situation by giving suggestions rather than telling them what to do.

Sample questions

- Write a letter to a new pupil who is starting at your school, giving advice about their first day.
- Write a letter to your past self, giving them recommendations about how to handle a difficult situation (real or imagined) you have been through.
- Write a letter of complaint to a phone company. Explain what went wrong but also how it should have been handled differently by the company.

Looking for more on this? Check out the writing section in Love and heartbreak on page 88.

Tips for improving

Modal verbs, such as 'could', 'might' or 'should', are really handy for this purpose.

Descriptive writing tasks

Being descriptive requires you to show off your language skills. Make sure you use language techniques, such as metaphor and simile, and also sensory description to make sure the reader feels like they are there. Small details make a big difference.

Sample questions

- Write a description of a walk in a forest.
- Describe an important historical place.
- Describe being in the middle of a storm.

Do you need more detail on description? Go back to the writing section in Conflict on page 154.

Tips for improving

Consider your structure too – pretend you are a film director and 'show' the reader the 'shots' you want them to see.

Discursive writing tasks

Discursive writing is like a spoken formal discussion, just in writing. You must provide a balanced approach to the topic, presenting both sides of the discussion. Planning is vital to this type of writing, so you know you have an equal amount of arguments on both sides. You should stay objective and unbiased throughout. A clear introduction, introducing the topic, and a strong conclusion, giving your own take on the topic, works well.

Sample questions

- Are exams the best way to judge children? Write a response to this question, discussing both sides of the debate.
- 'There should be more creative subjects in the curriculum.' Discuss.
- 'Computer games are dangerous.' Write an essay responding to this statement, considering both sides of the argument.

Looking for more on discursive writing? Turn back to Technology and communication on page 55.

Tips for improving

Using signpost words, like 'however' or 'on the other hand' and 'in addition' are useful for this type of writing.

Informative writing tasks

This is a straightforward type of writing in which you must inform your audience clearly and in detail. The task may ask you to 'describe' and, even though you want to show off your language skills, you must remember what the purpose is and not get carried away.

Sample questions

- Write a blog post, recommending a product or brand you really like. You should:
  - describe the product or brand
  - give recommendations about where to get it and how to use it.
- Write a news report about a recent school sports fixture (real or imagined).
- Write a report for your teacher about a recent trip you have been on. You should:
  - describe how you got there and back
  - describe what you saw and who you met
  - explain what you learnt.

Looking for more on informative writing? Turn back to Different people, different perspectives on page 137.

Tips for improving

If your task involves information about an event, using time connectives, such as 'after that' and 'subsequently', will help you to stay on track. If you're writing about a specific place or thing, you might use subheadings to organise your work too.

Narrative writing tasks

Narrative means 'story'. Writing a story does not mean you should use description though – you must show off your use of language techniques here too. Twists, extended metaphors or tension devices are great to include.

Sample questions

- Write a story entitled 'The Gift'.
- Write a narrative including the line 'and that was the end of that'.
- Write a story with one of the following titles:
  - 'The Storm at Sea'
  - 'A Walk in the Woods'
  - 'The Broken Glass'

Do you need revision on narrative writing? Turn back to Inventive inventions, page 105.

Tips for improving

Remember you're not writing a series of novels which will be turned into a film franchise! You won't have time to do that so start in the middle of the action and know where your story is headed.

Persuasive writing tasks

Writing with a purpose to persuade can be the most fun because you are writing from one point of view (usually yours) and using techniques to convince the reader, such as rhetorical questions, emotive language and quashing counter-arguments. A strong conclusion with an impactful statement makes a big difference when converting your reader. So, choose a task you feel strongly about.

Sample questions

- Write a speech persuading pupils in your school to elect you as School Captain.
- Write a letter of application for your dream job.
- 'There should be an age restriction of 16 and above on mobile phones.' Do you agree?

Need some practise with persuasive writing? Go back to the writing section in Our planet, page 39.

Tips for improving

Depending on the audience and form of the task, you must moderate the strength of your argument and judge whether you need to acknowledge and respect other points of view more carefully.

Planning and writing your responses
Ideas and structure

In this section, we will be looking at how to express yourself with clarity to show your understanding in all your written answers, but also with a bit of panache!

Responding to the task

In the writing exam, you will be marked on how you respond to the task. Here are some tips for **focusing on the task** at hand, whichever option you choose:

- Read the task carefully – highlight the key words in the task.
- Make sure you use the layout of the form. For example, for a letter, make sure your layout looks like a letter and you sign off appropriately at the end.
- Take care to consider the audience of your writing. For example, the audience of an article for a school magazine will be very different from a local newspaper.
- Think about how your piece of writing is delivered. For example, if it's a speech it will have audience who should be listening, but a blog post will be read.
- Use the words from the task in your writing, perhaps within the first or last line.

Planning

Planning is important so your ideas follow a logical and clear structure. In fact, you are encouraged in the exam to spend 10 minutes planning. Different people prefer different ways of planning but consider planning by paragraphs. Here is a brief example for a piece of narrative writing:

Paragraph 1 – set scene in house at the party

Paragraph 2 – move to the garden (Place)

Paragraph 3 – flashback to childhood (Time)

Paragraph 4 – someone from the party calls the narrator's name and

go back into present (Person)

In this example, you will see **TiP-ToP** paragraphing planning. This means that when the **T**ime, **P**lace, **T**opic or **P**erson changes, there is a new paragraph. This will help create an organised and effective structure, as well as using signpost connectives, of course.

Another mnemonic, **TAPF**, will also help you maximise the marks in this section. Before you write, consider the **T**one, **A**udience, **P**urpose and **F**orm of the task. This will help ensure the perspective you take and the **voice** and **register** you use will be suitable. For example, a letter written to your parents to persuade them to give you extra pocket money will be different in voice and register from a letter written to your headteacher about food waste at school mealtimes.

Language

You'll also be marked on your use of language.

Before you start writing, write a quick **checklist** or even your favourite mnemonic (such as **AFORREST** or **MAPSO**) at the top of your paper then tick it off as you use a technique. That way, you won't miss something.

Remember, even in non-fiction writing you can use **techniques** like metaphors and similes (they don't exclusively belong to fiction). The same is true of demonstrating a range of **vocabulary** and **sentence structures**, whatever the task. The key is to show off your language skills, not limit yourself!

Proofread carefully. You may want to proofread after each paragraph or as a complete text at the end, but remembering to look out for the Super Six will help:

> **Super Six proofreading tips**
>
> 1 **Spelling** – double check homophones like 'there', 'their', 'they're' as well as more complex words and words with a spelling pattern, such as double letters.
>
> 2 **Punctuation** – have you used a range correctly? Check you've included those pesky commas in direct speech.
>
> 3 **Capital letters** – proper nouns need capital letters, as do titles.
>
> 4 **Tense** – ensure you have maintained the same tense throughout.
>
> 5 **Person** – ensure you have maintained the same person throughout.
>
> 6 **TiP-ToP paragraphing** – add // where you have missed a new paragraph.

Not only should you be correcting but also improving. Can you use a better, more impactful word here? Could you use a semicolon instead there? Should you vary your sentence starters more?

Lastly, choose a task that excites you or you feel passionate about. It will come through in your writing.

Spelling, punctuation and grammar
Sentences

A sentence in its simplest form is created from a subject and a verb. For example, 'I walked.' More often than not, an object is added too. For example, 'I walked to the park.' When writing sentences or analysing sentences, it's important you know how they work.

There are three types of sentence:

● **Simple**, for example: *I walked to the park.*
● **Compound**, for example: *I walked to the park and I met my friend there.*
● **Complex** (sometimes called multi-clausal), for example: *I walked to the park and I met my friend there, which was nice because I hadn't seen them in ages.*

To make compound and complex sentences, you add more phrases and clauses.

● A **phrase** does not make sense make by itself and usually does not contain a verb. Here are some examples: 'a spoonful of sugar' (noun phrase), 'very slowly' (adverb phase), 'really excited' (adjective phrase), 'in front of the gate' (prepositional phrase).
● A **clause** sometimes makes sense by itself when it is the main clause of a sentence and sometimes not when it's a subordinate clause.

The chapters on Growing up, Journeying and Conflict have more information about sentence types.

Narrative voice – person

Imagine three people in a line. The first person introduces themselves, 'Hi, **I** am First Person.' The second person replies, 'Oh, **you** are First Person. You're famous!' Third Person is on the phone when they say, '**They** are here. First Person and Second Person, **he and she** are so straightforward!'

Here are some examples:

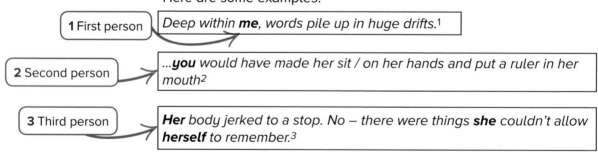

1 First person | *Deep within **me**, words pile up in huge drifts.*[1]

2 Second person | *...**you** would have made her sit / on her hands and put a ruler in her mouth*[2]

3 Third person | ***Her** body jerked to a stop. No – there were things **she** couldn't allow **herself** to remember.*[3]

Parts of speech

Knowing the parts of speech will not only help you identify them in sentences for **literal questions**, but also for **language effect** questions when you can discuss a word's function and the writer's intention by using it.

Revise the parts of speech and their functions using the table below:

Part of speech	Function	Examples	In context
Noun*	an object or thing	table / chair / book / love / hate	The **detective** strolled down the wet **street**.
Proper noun	the name of a place or person that needs a capital letter	Richard / London / Henrietta / Birmingham	The detective, called **Michelle**, strolled down the wet street.
Pronoun	use whichever pronouns suit the person (first, second or third) you are writing in	I / you / we / mine / yours / they / them	**I** strolled down the wet street, taking **my** time.
Adjective	a word that describes a noun	beautiful / painful / cold / astute / intelligent	The **determined** detective strolled down the **wet** street.
Verb	a word that describes a state of being or action	walking / sneezing / cooking / washing	The detective **strolled** down the wet street.
Adverb	a word that describes the manner, time or place of a verb. It often ends in -ly	carefully / above / always / slowly / quite / yesterday	The detective strolled **leisurely** down the wet street.
Connectives	words that connect sentences and signpost changes of thought	but / afterwards / so / and / furthermore / because	The detective strolled down the wet street **because** she had just left work.
Preposition	a word that shows you where or when something is in relation to another	after / under / on / before / inside / outside / from / since	The detective strolled **down** the wet street.
Imperative	a word that forms a command or request	Stop / don't go / please	**Watch out!** There's a detective on the street.
Determiner	determines how the noun or noun group is referenced	a / the / several / every / these / some	**Every** detective strolled down the wet street.
Articles / Definitive article	When used before a noun, 'the' defines it as something specific, whereas 'a' suggests there are several. It might show it is significant, possibly the only one of its kind, especially in poetry	A / An / The	**A / The** detective strolled down the wet street.

*Nouns can be categorised even further than this with abstract nouns (*peace*, *history*) collective nouns (*gaggle*, *herd*) and countable nouns (*beans*, *chairs*, *dogs*) to name a few. Here, we have put them together into one category for ease.

Tips for improving

Try choosing a long sentence from each book you read and identify as many parts of speech in it as you can. This will really help you gain confidence with parts of speech for the exam.

Formality

To show off your language skills at their best, stick to formal writing. That means avoiding **colloquial language** because it is too casual. Moreover, **clichés** and **idioms** will sound unoriginal unless absolutely necessary or if they help you develop your characters' speech. Look at the examples below and rewrite them in formal language.

At the end of the day, it's gonna be a tough game.

She's opened a can of worms by jabbering on and on about her mates.

Participles and tenses

Every verb has a present and a past participle.

- 'ing' is the **present participle**, for example: *dancing.*
- 'ed', 'en', 't' are **past participles**, for example: *danced, spoken, crept.*

We have to be careful with participles because you can use the same participle form when writing in different tenses. For example:

- *I am walking.* (**present participle** used in the **present progressive**)
- *I was walking.* (**present participle** used in the **past progressive**)

Homonyms and homophones

Homonyms sound the same, have different meanings and are spelt the same. For example:

- wear (*I wear socks*) / wear (*I will wear out my shoes with all this walking*)
- change (*I need to change my shirt*) / change (*I have enough change for a chocolate bar*).

Homophones sound the same, have different meanings but are spelt differently. For example:

- heard (*I heard a knock at the door*) / herd (*a herd of cows were in the field*)
- draft (*I must draft my essay*) / draught (*a cold draught blew through the house*)
- who's (*who's Ben?*) / whose (*whose book is this?*).

Sometimes it can help to work out what part of speech you need to use so that you use the right one. For example, 'effect' is usually a noun and 'affect' is usually a verb:

- *The medicine may affect how you feel.*
- *The effect of the medicine was immediate.*

Tips for other tricky spellings

The root word is the core of every word, so it usually won't change if you add a prefix or suffix. For example:

dis**appear**ed   **begin**ning   **embarrass**ment   **lone**ly   dis**agree**
de**finite**ly

Plurals can trip people up too, particularly with nouns that end in 'y'. Is it 'ies', 'es' or just 's'? Follow these simple rules to check:

● If there is a consonant before the 'y', for example 'baby', we change it to 'babies'.
● If there is a vowel before the 'y', for example 'journey', we just add 's', so 'journeys'.
● For any nouns that end in 'x' or 'ch', such as 'match', add 'es' to make 'matches'.

Look at page 122 in New kids for more on irregular plurals.

For words you find tricky, try creating a **mnemonic** to help you remember the spelling. Here are some examples:

● It is ne**cess**ary to have one **c**ollar and two **s**leeves on a **s**hirt.
● i before e except after c, for example: friend / receive.
● **r**hythm **h**elps **y**our **t**wo **h**ips **m**ove.

Imagining a tricky word in a **visual** way can help too.

For an example, check out the tip for remembering 'there' / 'their' / 'they're' on page 173.

Commas

Commas are used for adding extra information to a sentence, but they can be pesky punctuation. It can be very tempting to use them incorrectly by splicing a sentence. Sometimes this is called a run-on sentence and sometimes it is just completely wrong! For example:

Red pandas are not actually part of the panda family, they have their own classification.

Instead of splicing with a comma, you could use a connective, change the comma to a semicolon or make it two distinct sentences. Which one do you prefer?

● Red pandas are not actually part of the panada family **and** they have their own classification.
● Red pandas are not actually part of the panda family; they have their own classification.
● Red pandas are not actually part of the panda family. In fact, they have their own classification.

Go back to page 30 in Our planet for more on parentheses.

Dashes and brackets

Dashes and **brackets** can replace commas in a parentheses by adding more detail without cluttering up a sentence. But they can help you express your own writing style and tone too.

Dashes can act as asides, almost a whisper to a reader. The information in them helps in the understanding of a sentence and its writer or narrator. This can be because they include an opinion, which is why it is used in news writing, but they can also add humour. Here's an example:

The man in the grey suit – whose name I would later undoubtedly forget – shook my hand.

Think of brackets as more closed and secretive. The information they contain is not entirely necessary to understand the rest of the sentence and could possibly be skipped over by a reader. For example, it may contain a fact, which is helpful for non-fiction writing like this sentence:

Rosh Hashanah (the Hebrew name of the Jewish new year) usually takes place over two days during September.

Look at page 30 in Our planet for more on parentheses.

Tips for improving

Be careful not to clutter your writing by overusing dashes and brackets. Use them sparingly for real effect.

Colons and semicolons

You might think these punctuation marks are the most difficult, but they will not only 'show what you know' but also help you express your ideas in different ways. Here are some tips about how to use them:

- **Colons** can be used to replace a 'because':
  The baby elephant was alone: it had lost its herd.
- Colons can be used to start a list. Say how many things you are going to list for clarity:
  I went to the shop to buy three things: apples, bananas and carrots.
- **Semicolons** can be used to replace an 'and'. You don't need a conjunction when you use a semicolon:
  I saw the boat in the distance; I cried for help.
- Semicolons can be used to create a list of phrases:
  New York was amazing. It was full of vibrant, interesting people; diverse, eclectic neighbourhoods; and fantastically authentic food.

Look at page 14 in Growing up for more help with using this punctuation.

Apostrophes

Apostrophes can be annoying, but they only have two purposes so once we understand them, we have mastered them.

The first purpose is **contraction** (sometimes called **omission**). This is when two words are put together and letters are missed out. We often use this in speech and in less formal writing. Here are some examples:

- *Don't eat that! It's not healthy and we're about to have dinner.*
- *We've been to the museum, but they've changed the entrance fee.*

Turn back to page 127 in Different people, different perspectives for extra practice on this.

The second purpose is to show **possession** or ownership of something. For example:

- *Louise's cat*
- *Theo's book*

This one becomes tricky with words or plurals that end in 's' but there is a simple solution – put it on the end! For example:

- *the foxes' den*
- *Ms Jones' classroom*

Finally, when it comes to irregular plurals (such as 'people' or 'men' rather than 'person' or 'man') it is pretty simple too – just add an apostrophe and 's' as normal. For example:

- *the people's parliament*
- *the men's changing room*

Look back at page 162 in the Loud and proud chapter for more examples.

Tips for improving

Get into the habit of checking your writing for rogue apostrophes that may have crept in; for example, in 'its' when it means 'belonging to it' or in plurals like 'apples and pears'.

Direct and reported speech

There's an easy way to tell the difference between direct and reported speech: punctuation.

Direct speech: *'There's no way you're going to the park!' said Dad.*

Reported speech: *Dad said there was no way I was going to the park.*

That's why it's important to get direct speech punctuation correct. Here are a few things to get right when writing direct speech:

● New speaker = new line.
● Open and close your speech marks.
● All the punctuation related to what is said should be within the speech marks.
● Don't forget those commas after a reporting clause to introduce the line of speech.

Turn back to page 28 in Our planet for more examples and detail.

Tips for improving

Make sure you vary your synonyms for 'said' or add extra adverbs to describe how the character says the line.

Paragraphing

Structuring your writing in paragraphs will ensure your ideas are clearly presented and easy for a reader to engage with, whether you are analysing a poem, building tension in creative writing or providing different sides of an argument.

The mnemonic **TiP-ToP** can help you remember when to start a new paragraph. Start a new paragraph when the **Ti**me, **P**lace, **To**pic or **P**erson changes.

Turn back to page 44 in Technology and communication for more examples.

Tips for improving

If you forget to put in paragraphs, don't panic! At the end of the sentence where you would like a new paragraph, write //. This symbol lets a reader know that this is where a new paragraph should be.

Glossary

adjective   A word that describes a noun: *deep blue river*   **63**

alliteration   The occurrence of the same sound or letter at the beginning of consecutive or close words: *the birds were sweetly singing*   **19**

antonym   A word which has an opposite meaning to another: *hot* is the antonym of *cold*   **81**

apostrophes   A punctuation mark showing possession or omission of a letter / contraction of two words: *Ben's bicycle / Louise isn't here*   **127**

archetypal   Typical of a certain thing or person: *he is the archetypal villain*   **52**

asides   A dramatic device when a character speaks to the audience   **22**

assonance   repetition of vowel sounds in consecutive or close words: *the blinds were drawn down*   **19**

bias   An inclination towards one idea or the other, either favourably or unfavourably   **54**

call to action   A stimulus that induces the reader or listener to act   **38**

character   A person in a piece of literature or art   **9**

clause   A unit of a sentence, categorised as main clauses or subordinate clauses and separated by punctuation marks or conjunctions   **94**

complex sentences   A sentence with a main clause and a subordinate clause (or clauses): *Mrs Aubrey, an English teacher, marked the books.*   **94**

connotations   The associations of a word or thing; for example, associating the colour green with nature, newness or youth   **17**

counter-argument   An argument or reason that opposes another argument or idea   **31**

dashes   A punctuation mark that shows a pause or break: *You are my friend – my best friend – so I'd love to be your bridesmaid!*   **30**

description   A spoken or written account of a person, place or thing, often using rhetorical devices   **21**

dialogue   A written conversation between two or more people   **21**

direct speech   The reporting of what actual words are said by a speaker: *'I will go to the shop after dinner,' he said.*   **28**

discourse markers   A word or phrase that helps organise writing by acting as signposts for the reader, for example: *importantly / on the other hand / equally*   **47**

dystopian   Usually describing a piece of text that features an imagined future or society where there is great injustice or inequality   **26**

ellipsis   A set of three dots of punctuation that denote a pause or deliberate omission, often to add tension: *The distant howling rose and then fell...and then rose again.*   **95**

enjambment   The continuation of a line of poetry without pause over more than one line or stanza, denoted by a lack of punctuation   **84**

etymology   The origin of a word and its historical development   **55**

extended metaphor   The use of a single metaphor sustained at length; for example, a story about an avalanche in which the avalanche is compared to a dragon throughout   **84**

figurative (language / techniques)   Expression of ideas that goes beyond the literal by using figurative techniques, such as simile and metaphor   **71**

first person   A type of narrative when the protagonist tells their own story by using the pronouns 'I', 'me', 'my' and 'mine'   **78**

foreshadowing   A technique used by writers to give a clue or indicate a future event   **101**

hyperbole   Exaggerated statements that are not to be taken literally: *I have a million things to do today.*   **54**

idiosyncratic   Peculiar or individual way of doing things   **130**

implied   Meaning that is suggested, rather than explicit or obvious   **76**

instalment   A smaller segment of something that is to be broadcast, published or revealed at different times   **93**

inverted commas / speech marks   A punctuation mark that shows where speech or a quotation begins and ends. Can be used as double or single marks: *'Can you pass the salt?' said mum.* / *The phrase 'he clenched his fists' shows that he is angry.*   **28**

jump scare   An abrupt change in image or event that is meant to frighten the reader, listener or audience   **97**

language   The style of a piece of writing, including the vocabulary and techniques a writer uses   **21**

lyrical   Language or style that expresses the writer's emotions in an imaginative and beautiful way, often used in relation to poetry. Lyric poetry is derived from the Grecian period, when poetry was sung to a lyre's accompaniment   **33**

memoir   A historical account or biography written from personal knowledge   **20**

metaphor   A powerful image in which two different things or ideas are compared directly without using 'like' or 'as', for example: *the lake was a mirror*   **17**

mood   The atmosphere or feeling suggested by a piece of writing and felt by a reader   **48**

narrative drive   How a plot keeps a reader hooked and engaged through a sequence of events   **21**

narrative hooks   The opening of a piece of writing that engages the reader immediately   **70**

novella   A short novel or a long short story   **99**

object   The object of a sentence is the thing or person the action happens to, rather than what carries it out: *The boy kicked the ball.*   **12**

omniscient narrator   A third person narrator who seems to speak as the author because they are all-knowing, including the thoughts and feelings of the characters   **155**

onomatopoeia   The formation of a word from a sound associated with what is named: *The water gushed and splashed over the rocks.*   **19**

oxymoron   A figure of speech that describes something in opposing terms: *falsely true*   **81**

pace   The speed at which the information is told. Punctuation helps slow down or speed up writing   **22**

pathetic fallacy   When a writer reflects human emotions in natural features, such as the weather: *The grey, leaden mist hung low and heavy over the moor.*   **101**

plot   The main events of a story that take place in an interrelated order   **14**

power of three   Where three ideas are introduced together to enforce a point: *The holiday was spectacular, relaxing and outrageously expensive.*   **22**

prefixes   An affix at the beginning of word that changes the meaning of the root word, for example: ***dis**agree* / ***mis**understanding* / ***re**play*   **23**

protagonist   The leading character or one of the major characters in a piece of literature   **22**

pseudonym A false or fictitious name, usually used by an author to disguise their original name **76**

purpose An intention or reason, for example: to persuade, to inform, to describe **79**

register Variety of language determined by its informality or formality, evident in the use of vocabulary and syntax **120**

repetition The reoccurrence of something that has been written for emphasis **19**

reporting clause A clause that shows you are talking about what someone said or thought: *'I hate homework!' Amy shouted.* **28**

rhetorical question A question that is used for effect to make the audience or reader think: *Who doesn't want to save the world?* **37**

rhyme The correspondence of sound between words, particularly at the end of lines of poetry: *as the sun went down / the sky was pink across town* **35**

rhyme scheme The ordered pattern of rhymes at the ends of lines of poetry **84**

rhythm The measured flow of words and phrases determined by stressed and unstressed syllables **19**

second person A type of narrative when the reader is spoken to directly, using the pronouns 'you' and 'your' **190**

semantic field A set of words that can be categorised together; for example, 'brother', 'sister', 'mother' and 'father' are all in the semantic field of relations or family **133**

sequel Something that follows but is linked to the original, such as a book that develops or expands where the preceding book left off **93**

shape The physical shape a poem takes on a page, often linked to its meaning **35**

sibilance A form of alliteration specifically creating a hissing sound through the repetition of 's', 'sh', 'z': *the hissing snakes slithered and slunk* **54**

simile A vivid comparison of two things or ideas using 'like' or 'as', for example: *the lake was as still as a mirror* **17**

split direct speech The reporting of actual words said by a speaker, split by a reporting clause: *'I love this time of year,' said Lizzie, 'because the trees are such a beautiful colour.'* **28**

stage directions An instruction written in a drama script, suggesting how an actor should say something, how they should move or giving details about set or properties **52**

structure / structural devices The arrangement or construction of a piece of writing created by techniques, such as paragraphing **21**

subject The subject of a sentence is the thing or person that carries out the action, rather than what the action happens to: *The boy kicked the ball.* **12**

suffixes An affix at the end of word to form a different word, for example: *absolutely / powerful / mindless* **71**

symbols A thing or image that represents or stands for something else **17**

synonym A word that has the same or a similar meaning to another: *lukewarm is the synonym of tepid* **17**

syntax The arrangement of words and phrases to form a sentence **33**

third person A type of narrative when the narrator tells the story of characters by using the pronouns 'she', 'he', 'they' and 'them' **52**